Solving Sexual Problems
in the 1990s

American University Studies

Series VIII
Psychology

Vol. 15

PETER LANG
New York • Bern • Frankfurt am Main • Paris

Ben Neal Ard, Jr.

Solving Sexual Problems in the 1990s

PETER LANG
New York • Bern • Frankfurt am Main • Paris

Library of Congress Cataloging-in-Publication Data

Ard, Ben N.
    Solving Sexual Problems in the 1990s / Ben Neal
Ard, Jr.
    p. cm. — (American university studies. Series
VIII, Psychology ; vol. 15)
        Bibliograpy: p.
        Includes index.
        1. Sex customs—United States.   2. Sexual ethics—
United States.   3. Sex (Psychology)—United States.
I. Series: American university studies.   Series VIII,
Psychology ; v. 15
HQ18.U5A73   1989   306'.0973—dc19   88-37393
ISBN 0-8204-1061-6   CIP
ISSN 0740-0454

CIP-Titelaufnahme der Deutschen Bibliothek

Ard, Ben Neal:
Solving sexual problems in the 1990s / Ben Neal
Ard, Jr. — New York; Bern; Frankfurt am Main;
Paris: Lang, 1989.
    (American University Studies: Ser. 8,
    Psychology; Vol. 15)
    ISBN 0-8204-1061-6

NE: American University Studies / 08

© Peter Lang Publishing, Inc., New York 1989

Printed by Weihert-Druck GmbH, Darmstadt, West Germany

"The inescapable conclusion is that until our culture's attitudes toward sex undergo a change, there <u>cannot</u> be a satisfactory answer to the individual's sexual problems. It is not sex itself but people's attitudes toward it that give rise to these problems; and the sooner we realize that the real culprit is the attitude that we have about sex, the better off we will doubtless be."

Albert Ellis

(The American Sexual Tragedy, 1962, p. 293)

ACKNOWLEDGMENTS

When one wishes to acknowledge one' indebtness to others for what he has learned in a professional career, it soon becomes obvious that this poses a formidable problem. One cannot possibly list *all* the professors, supervisors, and significant others who have been influential. And in view of many peoples' reservations about dealing with sexual problems, I must confess that I have had many teachers, colleagues, and friends who have questioned my professional interest in sexual matters over my professional career. Many people are still suspicious of anyone who does research in the sexual area, or who publishes in the same area, or who tries in a professional scientific way to help people with sexual problems.

But a reader, it seems to me, is entitled to know up front from what sort of background a book is written. I think the background and prior experience of a writer had better be explicitly stated out the outset so that the reader will know from what sort of framework the writer offers his views. So I shall try to acknowledge some of my intellectual indebtedness to the many people who have helped me to get to the point from which this book is one result.

At the University of California at Los Angeles, where I earned my bachelor's degree in psychology (with a minor in philosophy), I was privileged to study abnormal psychology with Roy Dorcus, and habits (their making and unmaking) with Knight Dunlap, among others in psychology. Hans Reichenbach was a most influential philosopher and introduced me to scientific philosophy in several courses.

At the University of California at Berkeley, where I spent two years as a graduate student and research assistant, I first came into personal contact with Abraham Maslow (and learned about his studies of self-actualizing people) and also worked as an assistant to Harold E. Jones, as well as assisting in research projects involving, among other things, the secondary sexual characteristics of adolescent boys (a longitudinal study conducted at the Institute for Child Welfare).

Later at Oregon State University at Corvallis, where I earned my master of science degree (in counseling and psychology), I learned much about research in human sexual behavior as a byproducts of my master's thesis and in conjunction with my work as a graduate assistant to Lester A. Kirkendall.

Still later, while a fellow in marriage counseling and family life education at the Merrill-Palmer Institute in Detroit (thanks to the assistance of Robert A. Harper), I had a most intellectually stimulating year of supervised clinical experience. There I learned much about helping people from all walks of life, with all sorts of problems. There I had excellent supervision from Richard Kerckhoff, the late John Hudson, and Clark Moustakas. It was there that I also came into personal contact with various knowledgeable people who helped extend my knowledge beyond the limitations of my personal background and into the cross-cultural knowledge of anthropology, such people as Lawrence K. Frank, Dorothy Lee, Margaret Mead, and Ashley Montagu. I also had my first contact with Erich Fromm there.

While working on my doctorate (a Ph.D. across two departments: education and psychology) at the University of Michigan in Ann Arbor, I also had the good fortune to study philosophy with Walter Kaufmann, a renaissance man who taught me critical philosophy of the highest sort. I completed my doctoral research on the sexual behavior and attitudes of several hundred marital partners married twenty years (a longitudinal study) under the supervision of my major professor, E. Lowell Kelly (formerly chairman of the psychology department). Other members of my doctoral committee were Robert O. Blood, Allen Menlo, and Richard Kerckhoff.

Since my "formal" education was completed, I am happy to say that my continuing education has been very fruitful, with contacts at conferences, workshops, and in other meetings at various universities and colleges. I have had the good fortune to learn and share with the development of rational-emotive therapy over the years with Albert Ellis and Robert A. Harper. I have also enjoyed contacts with Wardell Pomeroy (of the famous Kinsey research team) and Owen Morgan, Clark Vincent, Gerhard Neubeck, Ira Reiss, William H. Masters and Virginia Johnson, as well as Harold Greenwald (who taught me the importance of humor in psychotherapy as well as his direct decision therapy).

Some of the evidence of my learning from these aforementioned scholars and clinicians will hopefully be somewhat revealed in the following pages, but the reader had better not assume that these people are to be held responsible for any misunderstandings on my part or necessarily for any of the conclusions I have drawn in this book. I must be accountable as a fallible human being for what I have learned and said herein. It is quite probable that some of these aforementioned people might well disagree with some of my statements and conclusions. Moreover, I hope the reader will not simply take any of my statements or conclusions "on faith" but will check them out against further scientific, empirical evidence. I have tried to offer contrasting points of view, even points of view that I personally disagree with, that is what I consider a scientific point of view.

Finally, I would like to acknowledge my debt to the students who have studied with me and thereby helped me as well as others learn more. Both undergraduate and graduate students have a way of asking questions that help everyone in the classroom or seminar think critically and learn more. I am grateful for this experience with students at several colleges and universities in the midwest and on the west coast.

And last, but by no means least, I would like to thank all those clients from various parts of the United States (and some from other countries) who brought their problems to me and worked hard on resolving them. I have endeavored not to reveal their confidences (by disguising some details); however, these sorts of problems are really very common, and therefore many people might imagine that they "see themselves" in these pages. Welcome to the human race. I hope that these patients' working through their problems will encourage others who may read this book to realize that such distress is resolvable in many instances. As an old saying puts it (and I have this framed and hanging in my office): Grant me the serenity to accept the things that I cannot change, the courage to change the things I can, and the intelligence to know the difference.

PREFACE

As we are approaching the 1990's and the 21st century, what with the "sexual revolution" (or the "sexual renaissance") and all the changing points of view regarding sex, what sorts of sexual problems can be anticipated and what sorts of professional help can be offered? I have been interested in studying sexology and providing professional help to people with sexual problems since the 1940's. I have lived and worked and taught in San Francisco since the 1960's and thus have witnessed and observed the counter-culture (hippie) movement, the feminist or women's liberation movement, and the gay liberation movement. All of these movements have influenced many of the ways people have looked at themselves and their sexual problems.

During this period, many books have been written and published on the subject of sex. There have been books on sex in the mass media, literature, theater, advertising, movies, TV, music, and so on. Many books have been written by and for physicians. Even an encyclopedia on sexual behavior has been published. Sex and the law has received much discussion. However, despite all this literature on sex, in our culture a large number of people continue to have sexual problems. The various helping professions can attest to this fact.

Many of the "popular" books that have been directed toward people with sexual problems have sometimes been none too helpful, for various reasons. For example, too many of these books have included myths, fallacies, and certain "values" (i.e., moral assumptions) which are ultimately detrimental to sound sexual functioning. Too many of the books by some physicians have frequently emphasized the medical aspects of sexual problems, focusing at great length on anatomy, physiology, and endocrinology, for example, to the point of seeming perhaps beyond the interests of many average or lay persons. Yet many, if not most, of the continuing sexual problems people have in our culture today (and looking ahead to the 1990's and the 21st century), are basically and fundamentally psychological and philosophical, rather than simply medical problems.

Sexual problems that many people have are frequently more a matter of attitudes, assumptions, values, philosophies, myths (e.g., old wives tales) and so on, rather than merely a matter of anatomy, physiology, or endocrinology. So what seems to be needed in this context is a book which deals with these basic causes of these perennial human sexual problems from a psychological and philosophical point of view.

These perennial human sexual problems are frequently centered not below the waist but rather above the neck. As the cognitive revolution has occurred in psychology in recent years, now psychotherapy can now realize that thinking (cognitive as well as conative factors) and behavior had better be recognized as a basic, fundamental part of human beings' reactions to sexual problems. Dr. Albert Ellis, in his founding of rational-emotive therapy (RET, for short) has provided psychotherapists with a most effective and elegant way of getting at the thinking aspect and the irrational ideas of human sexual behavior.

Despite the fact that some people think that we in this culture are going through a "sexual renaissance" if not a "sexual revolution" (or maybe because of it), many people still continue to have questions and problems about sexual matters. Our culture has many puritanical and even victorian ideas (derived from the Judeo-Christian religious teachings and assumptions) which are still prevalent and which cause sexual problems to this day (and probably will still continue to do so into the 21st century). This is one of the reasons why a book which discusses sexual problems from a rational, scientific, humanistic, philosophical point of view would seem to serve a real need as we look to the future from this point in time.

The present book is therefore offered to the serious-minded adult who wants a brief introduction to some more rational methods of handling sexual problems from a psychological and philosophical point of view. It is written in everyday language for the most part, instead of technical jargon. While the book is based on the latest scientific research findings, there will not be the usual dry, boring statistics and endless citations in footnotes to obscure research studies. Each chapter will discuss a common set of sexual problems (or problem area), and offer some suggestions as to how an intelligent person can learn to reorient his or her thinking, if she or he has similar problems. At the end of each chapter will be found a bibliography as suggested further readings for the person who wishes to delve a bit deeper into this particular area. These bibliographical items are representative of a wide variety of points of view and offer scientific evidence for various point of view, opposing and contrasting as well as views with which I personally disagree. So I say to the reader, don't take my word for anything, check it out by reading the scientific, verifiable, empirical literature.

Obviously, if the problem persists, a person may wish to consult more professional help of a more personal sort to help rid himself or herself of the problem through counseling or psychotherapy. Possible referral resources are mentioned at the end of the book. But many of these sorts of sexual problems can be alleviated or resolved to a great extent frequently by reading (bibliotherapy) and reorienting one's self-defeating irrational ideas, values and assumptions. This book can help to do just that if the reader will read it critically and thoughtfully and try out some of the ideas suggested that might apply to his or her particular problems.

The person who would like a broad but brief introduction to the kinds of problems people have (and probably can be expected to continue to have in the 1990's and the 21st century), may profitably use this book as a starting reference. He or she may wish to keep it as a reference to consult concerning particular sexual problems as life progresses, since the book has chapters which cover concerns and difficulties from youth through the later years.

This book includes suggestions which have been used in the author's private practice as a psychologist, marriage counselor and sex therapist. If the suggestions are considered as worth trying in the reader's personal life, the reader can begin to unlearn some of the self-defeating, irrational ideas, values and assumptions and thereby integrate sex into his or her life in a more productive, self-actualizing, humanistic, and rational way.

Ben Neal Ard, Jr., Ph.D.

San Francisco
1989

CONTENTS

"Were life more sensual it would be more good! And yet we still so often start our babies off in a world where we are half ashamed of suckling, half disgusted by excretion, half afraid of nakedness, and more than half ashamed of sex.

We can neither be sensual ourselves nor allow others their sensuality. Neither enter the heaven of our earth, nor let those others in. So, having despised the lower, we seek fretfully and vainly for what we call the 'higher' things. Having poisoned the soil in which they grow we rail against the bitterness of the fruit."

Grace Stuart
Conscience and Reason (1951, p. 202)

CHAPTER 1

FACTS AND FALLACIES ABOUT SEX:
CHANGING IDEAS ABOUT SEX

There are many popular notions about sexual matters which get in the way of effective sexual functioning. This whole book may be said to be a discussion of just such matters in one sense, but this particular chapter will deal briefly with some common presumptions which cause difficulty in sexual relations, and also present the facts that are needed to correct these misconceptions.

When young people begin to grow up and become concerned about interacting with the other sex, their notions about sex and related matters can affect their overall adjustment. Two areas will be discussed as illustrations: petting and drugs. Young people (as well those older) today have many fallacious notions about both of these subjects.

As young people first begin to get involved in sexual matters, one of the first areas where ideas begin to come into play which may have a positive or negative effect on sex is that of petting. Will petting help or harm future marriage adjustment, specifically sexual adjustment in marriage?

The times, they are achangin' (in many ways), and as far as sexual behavior is concerned, perhaps the greatest changes are seen with respect to petting. There are many people, of course, who still feel today that any petting before marriage is wrong and sinful. But an increasing number of people are taking a more liberal view about petting.

What is a rational position to take on petting? Do "nice" girls pet?

What do boys expect? What actual harm does petting in itself do? Before dealing with these questions, perhaps a definition of just what petting means is in order.

For our purposes, petting may be taken to mean any caressing or fondling of a girl by a boy, usually below the neck, with the intent of sexual arousal or satisfaction. Now obviously a girl can "pet" a boy, too (and many modern girls do), but the initiative is traditionally thought of as belonging to the male in our culture.

In the old days "nice" girls would never allow any petting. Even mere kissing or "necking" was limited to the engagement period. But necking and petting have come into wider acceptance among high school and college youth and some form of petting now occurs among nearly all youth. The question of how far to go is the main issue today among all but the devoutly religious.

So nice girls today do pet, at least a large percentage do. But some will draw the line at various parts of the body being caressed. What is "acceptable" to young women today as far as petting is concerned varies according to their assumptions of what is permissible and with whom. When "in love" with a boy they think they are going to marry (or have a long-term, serious relationship with), more petting is usually permitted. In general, there seems to be a trend toward more premarital petting. The psychology of relations between the sexes (the rating and dating game) may be paraphrased as: girls want love, and use sex to get it; boys want sex, and talk of love to get it. Thus the battle between the sexes goes on.

Most young people who pet, even those who pet the most extensively, rarely talk out their views about petting beforehand with the other sex. Boys frequently expect to try and go as far as they can with petting, and thus "score" or "make out." Girls frequently try to permit as little petting as possible and still keep the boy coming back. Who wins in such a situation is hard to see, since there is a fundamental dishonesty here which is rarely candidly faced.

Other factors contributing to the absurdity of this situation are that the girl may dress and act as seductively and as sexy as possible, supposedly to attract the other gender; but then, when her actions are successful and the boy responds and attempts some petting, she may appear to be highly insulted by his sexual overtures and accuse him of not respecting her! Despite the obvious irrationality here, such scenes occur on many a lover's lane nearly every Saturday night across the land.

On the other hand, if a young man respects a girl very much and does not want to offend her, he may not try any petting. Then, as absurdity builds on dishonesty, the girl may think the boy does not like her because he "didn't make a pass." So it seems that many nice girls want boys to make an attempt at some petting, but not go "too far." And boys frequently try to go as far as they can in petting, with the implied assumption that it is all up to the girl to set the limits.

Some girls will even allow much more petting with a boy they are not involved with than with a boy they think they might marry. Such girls assume that their potential mate will not think they are "nice" if they permit too much petting. Such are the absurd lengths to which some people will go because of their irrational, contradictory attitudes toward sex.

What harm does petting do? Petting as a prelude to sexual intercourse is normal and natural and can cause no harm in and of itself.

However, a pattern of premarital petting which always stops short of orgasm can lead to unfortunate consequences for both men and women.

One young married woman, coming in for marriage counseling because she was having trouble responding to sexual intercourse, was able to trace the beginning of her troubles to a pattern of premarital petting wherein she and her future husband petted but always stopped short of sexual intercourse or orgasm. She came to feel that a "wall" existed beyond which she was not to go. The wall was preventing her from enjoying sexual intercourse in her marriage. Presumably if she had established a pattern of petting as a natural prelude to sexual intercourse, or had petted to orgasm, her difficulties would not have arisen in the first place.

Premarital petting which is never a prelude to sexual intercourse, and is never continued until orgasm is achieved, can be very frustrating to both men and women and may result in unpleasant states of tension, pains in the groin or testicular region, headaches, and other signs of physical discomfort. Prolonged petting without ever getting any release through orgasm may result in pelvic congestion which might lead to ailments of the genital tract, according to some authorities.

When premarital petting is practiced exclusively as a means of achieving orgasm (with sexual intercourse avoided at all costs), it may prove to be a form of compulsiveness which is very self-defeating. Where no birth control methods are immediately available, or where there is danger of VD or STD's (sexually transmitted diseases), a woman may rationally choose to pet to orgasm rather than have sexual intercourse on a given occasion. However, these reasons appear less compelling in these days of birth control pills, condoms, vasectomies, etc. Nevertheless, some women are illogically and irrationally afraid of sexual intercourse, or compulsively concerned about the technical loss of their virginity; such women sometimes use petting exclusively for their orgasmic release.

On the other hand, if more young men practiced a wider variety of premarital petting techniques, it might help out later on in their marriages. If a young man has petted with a variety of women and has learned that a variety of techniques are necessary to stimulate and satisfy different women, he is in a better position to help his wife achieve orgasm. And if women learn to accept and enjoy someone fondling and caressing various parts of their body, they will probably have a better sexual adjustment in marriage.

In America there is still considerable hesitancy about touching. And yet in making love, touching is the essence of adequate sexual functioning. Many married couples, even after having had sexual intercourse regularly for many years, are still not able to communicate very well with each other about how they want their loving done.

Premarital petting which is openly and honestly arrived at, rather than being a cop-out, can serve as an excellent learning experience. It can help people learn about their own bodily responses, how to let themselves go, how to relax, what they particularly enjoy, what excites them and brings sexual satisfaction. All of these facts are an important part of sex education and cannot be left entirely to books.

Some practical experience in premarital petting can serve to make both men and women more knowledgeable and thoughtful lovers in their later marriages and thus contribute to their sexual enjoyment as well as to their pleasure in giving and receiving love and affection. If petting is resorted to out of irrational fears of sexual intercourse, then it may tend to be self-

6

defeating.

Because many young people are anxious and nervous about their first efforts at interaction with the other sex, be it petting to orgasm or actual sexual intercourse, some young men and women have been turning to drugs in the vain hope that these drugs will help them have more satisfactory sexual interactions with the other sex. The whole area where sex and drugs interface is one filled with misconceptions and distorted beliefs, as well as unrealizable expectations.

Humans have for many years sought various drugs which they hoped would help in the performance or enjoyment of sex. Probably from the time that humans were taught that sex is dirty, evil, and sinful, there have been people who have had difficulty in the sexual areas of their life. Out of these negative teachings have developed inhibitions, repressions, myths, and fallacies about sex which have interfered with the enjoyment and performance of sexual acts. Because of these difficulties with sex, and the many false assumptions about it, people have frequently turned to some "crutch" to hopefully help them perform better in the sexual area. And drugs of various kinds have been assumed (erroneously) to be helpful in many ways. ("Drugs" in this context may refer to any biologically active substance used in the treatment of illness by the medical profession, or bought "on the street" for recreation or pleasure.)

Aphrodisiacs are drugs or substances which people assume will excite sexual desire or aid in sexual performance. Despite many old wives' tales about various foodstuffs (caviar, oysters, garlic, and so on) and various drugs (marijuana, alcohol, LSD, "Spanish fly," and so on), there are actually no drugs or foodstuffs that have been scientifically proven to be true aphrodisiacs.

A lot of people <u>claim</u> that they have had an experience with some drug that proved to them that they could perform sex better. But the scientific evidence is still that *there are no drugs which act as true aphrodisiacs* (that is, that will regularly and consistently improve sexual performance in all people where the drugs are administered under a variety of circumstances). The scientific evidence is that effects are inconsistent and usually secondary to other factors.

Marijuana and LSD have *erroneously* been thought by many people to aid their sexual performance. Both of these drugs are found to have a variety of effects on people in the sexual area. The psychological "set" of the persons taking these drugs (that is, their expectations, what they have been led to believe) affect the reactions they get. Also, the setting, the circumstances, the people with whom the drugs are taken, all affect the reactions. People who have had a "good" sexual experience after taking marijuana or LSD assume that the drug caused the superior sex. Such is not consistently the case as far as any scientific evidence is concerned, however.

As an illustration, in my private practice as a psychologist, marriage counselor and sex therapist, one male client reported that he had "great sex" with his "old lady" (girl friend) *only when they were high on LSD together.* When neither one took LSD they could not stand each other. Now in a brief vignette we cannot go into the details such as the number of sessions it might take to resolve this matter, but the ultimate logical alternatives here would seem to be: stay high on LSD henceforth (in order, presumably, to have "great sex"), or, find another partner with whom it might be possible to have good sex *without* any drugs. Since no drug, including LSD, is a reliable aphrodisiac, the choice should be obvious. But many people still look for what they think is the easy way out.

Alcohol has been erroneously assumed by many people to be a sexual stimulant. In fact it is not. It may reduce some inhibitions but it also weakens sexual performance. So many a man has fallen into a self-made trap when he has tried to ply a woman with alcohol (in order to get her to have sex with him); the drinks they both have had may have reduced some of their inhibitions and they then retired to bed, only to find that the alcohol is more likely to interfere with their sexual performance rather than contribute to an outstanding sexual performance. Alcohol actually is a depressant rather than a stimulant. It is an anesthetic, in fact. Alcohol actually blocks the neural pathways that govern erection, thus causing temporary impotence.

"Spanish fly" is a layman's term for a drug which is assumed (erroneously, again) to arouse sexual desire in women, but which actually causes itching and irritation in the genitourinary tract (specifically the mucous membrane of the urethra). The drug (cantharides), which is derived from a beetle, can actually cause violent illness and even death, if taken in excessive doses. Once again, a drug which is supposed by some people to arouse sexual desire (and thus be an aphrodisiac) does not do the job people assume it will do. Folklore is not a good thing to follow; scientific evidence proves more reliable than what may be heard from various people who do not know what they are talking about.

No drugs can be said to be specific aphrodisiacs in that none of them would consistently intensify sexual desire if given to a variety of people in many different settings. *Science* rather than superstition, folklore, old wives' tales or occult knowledge, is the best and most reliable source of what effects various drugs have on sex.

Dr. Joel Fort, a nationally acclaimed physician specializing in social psychiatry and drug abuse, has stated that "Excessive doses of sedative or depressant drugs, such as alcohol, barbiturates, or narcotics, ordinarily diminished sexual performance, thus having an anaphrodisiac or anti-sexual effect." (Fort, 1969, p. 137) Dr. Fort has also pointed out that narcotic addiction, alcoholism, and other types of drug abuse usually are accompanied by greatly diminished sexual interest and performance, impotence, and sometimes sterility.

The "psychedelic" drugs in general do _not_ promote sexual desire and do _not_ excite the sexual organs. These are the facts from a scientific point of view. And yet many people still falsely assume that such drugs will "turn on" sex and practically provide a sexual Nirvana.

If anyone has difficulties with sex, rather than seeking help from the "street scene" with its erroneous assumptions about drugs, it would seem far better to get at the underlying causes of the sexual difficulty from the best scientific assistance obtainable. Counseling or psychotherapy are more likely to turn up such things as feelings of guilt, inhibitions, unquestioned assumptions, moralistic ideas, and the like. Counseling and psychotherapy are therefore ultimately better to turn to, rather than street drugs, for problems relating to sex. The reputed relationship between street drugs and sex is just one more myth that we had better get rid of and replace with more scientific, realistic ideas that will be less self-defeating.

There are many myths about sex that are not related to drugs, and they need to be exploded, too. Some of these have already been exploded in scientific circles (Salzman, 1970), but some linger on in old wives' tales, folklore, the mass media, and other areas where sex is not looked at scientifically. Sex being identified with "sin" in our culture's religions encouraged ignorance and myth making.

Some of the myths in the sexual area may be traced back to some of the writing of Sigmund Freud, the founder of psychoanalysis. While he pioneered in the investigations of sex in human behavior, he also perpetuated some notions which later have had detrimental effects on the sexual adjustment of many human beings. His notions about supposed male supremacy (or primacy), penis envy on the part of the female, the supposed omnipotent libido (or sexual instinct), the assumed universality of the oedipal complex, the so-called death instinct, the "latency" period, some of his ideas about the superego, and many other ideas had better be looked at in the light of more recent scientific knowledge, rather than swallowed whole merely because Freud said it. While it will not be feasible to examine each of these ideas in the present context, a few will be discussed here, and others in later chapters.

One of the myths that still influence some people today is that of a sex-linked character structure. Freud extrapolated way beyond the biological facts when he related sexual behavior, roles and functions of the sexes, and an identification of certain behaviors that were "appropriate" to men and others to women to "character structure." Recent scientific findings have demonstrated that sex and character structure (or masculinity and femininity) are not as biologically ordained as previously thought by the Freudians; on the contrary, many of the differences between male and female behavior are *culturally derived* (and therefore are alterable, not just biologically given). For example, the old notion that the female is *inherently passive* while the male is *inherently active* (or aggressive) has been shown to be fallacious. Modern women are exploding this particular myth every day, to the surprise (and sometimes delight) of *some* men. The common assumption that the male must always be the active one, the instigator in sexual matters, while the female must always be passive (because it is her "nature," presumably, according to this argument), is simply not valid. *Both* partners in the sexual act and in the foreplay can be passive *and* active at different times, and this makes the sex act the mutually cooperative sort of functioning that it can delightfully be -- if both partners can unburden themselves of some of the old myths about male and female sexuality.

Probably one of the more unfortunate and groundless myths that Freud was responsible for (and one that is supposed to make females feel inferior) is that the female has an envy of the male penis. This "penis envy" concept of Freud's is felt by many modern women to be insulting to females. As a matter of fact, the woman is in some ways better equipped to enjoy sex more fully and more easily than a man is. That is, she can have sex more readily, not needing the tumescence or desire to the same degree that men seem to; she can have successive multiple orgasms more quickly than a man can in general; she can return to sex more quickly than her male partner can (that is, the male, in general requires a refractory period before further orgasms are possible for him); and so forth.

Although Freud thought of sex (or the libido, to use his term) as an instinct, most behavioral scientists today do *not* regard sex as instinctual in human beings (if we use the term instinct properly as it is used among the sciences of psychology and zoology today). More emphasis today is put on the *learned* aspects of the sexual drive, particularly as we move up the phylogenetic scale from the lower animals to human beings. The libido theory Freud postulated also perpetuated many needless related assumptions, such as the one that all reactive activities are ultimately the product of *sublimation*. Freud's theory of sublimation, while attractive to religious leaders for obvious reasons (they are frequently so essentially anti-sex) really has little scientific evidence to substantiate the concept.

Still another myth perpetuated by Freud's psychoanalytic speculations was that of "latent homosexuality" or a homosexual stage of development in all individuals. This concept is tied up with another Freudian myth: that all human beings are *bisexual* by nature. These notions can no longer be accepted as fact. As Salzman (1970, p. 203) has noted, the concept of bisexuality is strongly disputed by most biologists and its application to humans is highly doubtful. However, the myth that every individual has both homosexual and heterosexual traits dies very slowly, unfortunately. More about these concepts will be discussed in some detail in a later chapter. While Freud taught us a lot about sex, and was one of the early leaders in the study of the influence of sex upon human beings, his works have unfortunately been passed on as dogma rather than as hypotheses to be checked out and verified as tenable or not.

Hopefully, today we can, so to speak, stand on Freud's shoulders and see much further than he did. Science, and particularly sexology, has made much progress since his day, particularly with anthropological data from cross-cultural studies of men like Kinsey, Pomeroy, the Ellises (both Albert and Havelock), Kirkendall, and Reiss; of Margaret Mead and other anthropologists; plus the research of Masters and Johnson, we have come a long way from the original insights and speculations of Sigmund Freud in 19th century Vienna. (Ard, 1954)

In the following chapters, typical, as well as some unusual, problems that many people have with sex will be discussed in some detail. In this chapter, an attempt has been made to establish a point of view which maintains that some people hold many fallacious ideas about sex, some derived from religious teachings, some from hearsay, and some even from professionals like Sigmund Freud. A more critical, rational and humanistic look at human sexuality would seem to be needed and will be attempted in the following chapters.

SUGGESTED FURTHER READING

Ard, Ben N., Jr. "Needed Research in Selected Areas of Human Sex
  Research." Unpublished Master's thesis, Oregon State University,
  Corvallis, 1954.

Ard, Ben N., Jr. "Petting: Will It Harm or Help Future Marriage?"
  Sexology, 32 (1966), 781-785.

Ellis, Albert. "Thoughts on Petting." in Albert Ellis, *Sex Without Guilt*
  (New york: Lyle Stuart, 1958).

Ellis, Albert. *The Folklore of Sex* (New York: Grove Press, revised edition,
  1961).

Fort, Joel. *The Pleasure Seekers: The Drug Crises, Youth and Society*
  (New York: Grove Press, 1969).

Harper, Robert A. "Petting." in Albert Ellis and Albert Abarbanel (Eds.),
  The Encyclopedia of Sexual Behavior (New York: Hawthorn Books,
  1961), volume 1, pp. 812-818.

Salzman, Leon. "Recently Exploded Sexual Myths." in Donald L. Taylor
  (ed.) *Human Sexual Development* (Philadelphia: Davis, 1970), pp.
  194-204.

Stuart, Grace. *Conscience and Reason*. New York: Macmillan, 1951.

"At bottom, the sabotaging of human sex-love relations is a problem which is socially rather than individually created, and which therefore cannot be solved on a broad scale without wide-spread societal changes in sex attitudes."

Albert Ellis
The American Sexual Tragedy
(1954, pp. 264-265)

CHAPTER 2

IMPROVING BODY IMAGE AND SEXUAL ATTITUDES

A very important part of all persons' adequate sexual functioning is their attitude toward their own bodies and those of the other sex. Our culture builds into too many people unfortunate attitudes that result in self-defeating behaviors and feelings. The culture also emphasizes youth and good looks in the movies and on television as well as in advertising and the various other mass media. Beauty or handsomeness is obviously related to sex, but the relationship is not as simple as the films and TV would have us believe.

As illustrations of the sort of self-defeating ideas young mean and women can and do develop in our culture, consider the ideas many women have about their breasts and the notions many men have about their penises. Ideas about what is "proper" with regard to such matters can cause considerable difficulties.

One of the most common complaints many men have with regard to sexual matters is that their penises are too small and that, therefore, they will not be able to perform the sexual act adequately. These males assume that a large penis is absolutely necessary to satisfy any woman.

Many older men, even after being married for many years, still feel inadequate, thinking they fail to satisfy their wives because their penises are inadequate. And there are many men who never marry because they feel their penises are insufficient for them to ever function sexually with a woman; so they refrain from ever risking themselves sexually with a woman.

All of these worries about penis size share a common underlying misconception. This is the mistaken belief that a large penis is necessary for an adequate sexual performance. Such a belief is simply not based upon fact. Part of this common misconception that adequate sexual performance depends upon a large penis may be traced to a lack of understanding of the anatomical relationships in sexual intercourse. If people really understood just what happens in sexual intercourse, these popular fears would be greatly reduced.

Basically, the female vagina is so constructed that it stretches to accommodate whatever size penis is inserted. This is practically a foolproof arrangement as far as genital size is concerned. It assures that -- even when large men marry small women, or vice versa -- genital size will be a relatively unimportant matter in all but a very small number of cases.

In addition, the inside of the female vagina is not very sexually sensitive. It is the outer part, including the labia (lips) and clitoris - the vulva - that are sexually excitable. Thus, the size of the penis is of no basic significance in arousing and satisfying a woman.

Many young men typically get their impressions of having a "small" penis during adolescence when they compare themselves with other boys in the locker-room shower at the gym, perhaps after a basketball game. There always seem to be other fellows around who have larger genitals. The factor of selective attention seems to be involved in the young boys noticing the fellows who are larger than they rather than the ones who are smaller. So "impressions" rather than scientific evidence prevails.

Part of this reaction may, of course, be due simply to a delayed development on the part of the observer. Some boys develop pubic hair and complete their genital maturation earlier than others. But the "victim" or observer does not realize that, although boys his own age may be ahead of him in development at a particular moment in time, he will usually catch up with them - unless of course there is some endocrine (or hormone) problem, a relatively rare occurrence. But the average penis is five and one half to six inches, and practically all men approximate that size.

The main thing to remember is that genital size does not determine the adequacy of sexual performance. The young man who compares himself with others in the shower room and thinks that, because he apparently has smaller genitals, he is therefore somehow "less of a man" is simply making a mistake in his thinking.

Another miscalculation he may be making is in overlooking the fact that there is no exact relationship between the limp or flaccid penis and its size when erect. A small penis may get much larger at erection, so that it equals or rivals one that is larger when not erect. A man's ability to satisfy a woman in the sexual act does not depend on the size of his penis. The sooner we get rid of this notion the better off everyone will be. Both men and women had better learn this basic fact.

The most important factor in sexual performance is emotional attitude, or the way one thinks about sexual matters. As a matter of simple fact, a man can bring a woman to sexual orgasm without using this penis at all. In this instance, as with others in sexual relationships, knowing how to use one's hands is at least as important, if not more so, than exploiting one's penis.

The quality of the emotional or interpersonal relationship between a man and a woman is a great deal more important than penile size in

22

determining what sort of a sexual relationship they will have. An attentive and thoughtful man with a basic knowledge of sexual anatomy and psychology, who has a healthy attitude and is willing to try different things in his lovemaking, will be able to satisfy his sexual partner in most instances.

Timing in lovemaking also overshadows genital size. A man's being sensitive and thoughtful and aware of his partner's feelings, desires, and responses are matters which make more of a difference to a woman than the size of her partner's genitals.

Since neither overall physical size, nor the size of man's penis, are related in any significant way with his ability to perform adequately in a sexual relationship, these false ideas need to be attacked, demolished, and removed from one's mind as ultimately self-defeating and not in accord with the facts. Any man who has any doubts about this had better check it out.

Many men are often so embarrassed about the supposedly small size of their penises, however, that they will not even check out the facts with a physician, sexologist, psychologist, or marriage counselor. These experts could reassure a man about his worries in this regard if he would only summon enough courage to talk about them.

Too many men seem to feel that raising any question about sexual matters with a professional person is an indication that they themselves do not know about sex. And this seems to be very hard for many men to admit.

But to admit that one is willing to learn more about any area, particularly the sexual, is surely a sign of mental health and maturity, rather than weakness. And when one has false ideas about so important an area as the sexual, it is certainly worth talking about with someone who has been trained to help in such matters.

Such a specialist can help a man get rid of any misconceptions about sex that he may have. Ultimately, of course, every man has to root such self-defeating ideas out of his own head, but talking it over with a professional person can often be the first helpful step.

Some self-help is possible, of course. By reading books and magazines and checking one's ideas out (and keeping an open mind), one can begin to challenge, change, and get rid of self-defeating worries, particularly the false idea that the size of man's penis determines how well he can function sexually.

*　　　*　　　*

The analogous worry among women seems to be about their breast size. Apparently few physical features can be as disturbing to a woman as breasts which she thinks are the wrong size. And such worries in our culture may start at a surprisingly early age.

An eight-year-old girl, taking her bath as her mother disrobed within the girl's view, suddenly burst into tears. When the mother asked what was the matter, the girl looked down at her own body and then at her mother's more mature figure and blurted out: "It's just that I'm so plain, and you're so fancy."

This incident illustrates how some girls' worries begin. They are frequently too concerned about their breasts. Many counselors, physicians, and psychologists who have gained the confidence of women clients frequently hear complaints from females of various ages that their breast are "not right"; they are either "too large" or "too small," *they think*. Few women seem to be satisfied with their breasts these days, it would seem.

Some women become overconcerned about their breasts when they have children. They fear that having children, and particularly breast-feeding them, will adversely affect their breasts. Sometimes they fear their breasts will become smaller.

It is not true that in most cases when a woman has a child the breasts get smaller. The way the baby is weaned is important, however. If the breasts are allowed to become filled with milk, so that some of the fatty tissue around the breast is broken down, and the little suspending ligaments are also stretched too much, the breasts may droop and hang. But if the child is weaned slowly and carefully and the woman maintains her own body weight, the breasts may retain their size and shape.

Perhaps gaining some perspective on this matter of breast size will help. "Styles" in breast size have evidently changed over the ages as much as the fashion in women's clothes. During different periods of history, women's breasts have been either covered up or revealed. In America, one has only to remember the changes in clothing styles from the flapper period, when women wore binders to flatten their breasts, to the sweater-girl days of Lana Turner, and finally to the see-through blouses and the bra-less fashions today.

Times do change. Now many women seem to feel that they are not adequate if they do not have breasts like some of the well-publicized film stars. What can be done about this problem?

There are several approaches to the problem of breast size, which seemingly concerns many women these days. Essentially these may be termed the medical, the exercise, the brassiere, and the psychological approaches.

General body build is inherited, although a woman's figure is obviously affected by her diet, childbearing, and other factors. An endocrinologist (a physician specializing in hormone problems) may need to be consulted in some cases where too much or too little hormone may have affected breast size and breast shape. But this is rather rare.

Growths in the breasts may cause some enlargement, perhaps requiring surgery. Such growths should be checked by a physician. But surgery merely to alter the size of breasts (i.e., to enlarge them) is practically never desirable. Such operations can increase the size of breasts by the insertion of material (e.g., silicone). Of course any mature woman is entitled to such extreme methods if she wishes. But she should know that most medical men do not recommend these operations. In many cases the material hardens and must be removed later. If a woman has a healthy attitude, there is really no justifiable reason to go to all the expense of such surgery.

Many women, unhappy with what they consider to be small breasts, turn to ads in various magazines to find a solution to their problem. Many quacks and fly-by-night advertisers cash in on this overconcern with breasts among many women and have offered phony gimmicks that cannot help a woman gain larger breasts.

Exercise of a particular sort, some say, may help a woman keep full breasts firm. To some extent exercises may help posture and carriage, but the exercise approach cannot realistically be expected to change the size of breasts.

Most women had better come to accept the fact that there is no assurance through hormone creams or exercises that they can attain the particular size of breasts they desire. It is when they perhaps have exhausted these two approaches and have been unsuccessful that they may turn to the brassiere approach.

Brassieres with padding ("falsies") can provide a bustline more to the woman's liking. And if looking good in certain clothes is all that a woman wants from the wearing a brassiere padded with "falsies," this can easily be achieved.

However, many women wear falsies to attract men, frequently feeling that they are somewhat less feminine or less sexually attractive if they do not measure up to the Hollywood standard of a "perfect 36." It is the feeling of insecurity that sometimes accompanies the wearing of falsies that may call forth the need for the psychological approach.

A woman had better recognize that she is acceptable and lovable as an individual, *whatever* her breast measurements may happen to be. This is fundamentally the best approach to overconcern about breasts.

Sexual competence is much more a matter of *attitudes* than it is a matter of figure or breast measurements. Once women realize this, and really accept it completely, they can relax and concentrate on the more important aspects of being good sexual partners. In other words, they had better concentrate their thinking, on changing their attitudes toward sex, including accepting their own standard equipment. Self-defeating attitudes (particularly inhibiting attitudes) can be changed. Of course, professional help and advice may sometimes be indicated.

Tape measures can never measure one's worthwhileness as a person, or one's competence in bed. This is true both for women and men. This means that the most important thing that makes a woman sexually attractive in the long run is her outlook toward sex, toward herself, and toward men, *not* her breast measurements.

The psychological approach is thus more fundamental; it bypasses the secondary aspects of breast measurements and breast shapes and gets down to the more basic matter in sexual relations: *attitudes.* And these, if they are self-defeating, by the way, are changeable.

So far we have been considering body image which is largely self-image, that is, men's worries about their penises and women's worries about their breasts. But there are also concerns and misconceptions about body image which refer to the other sex. That is, the relationship of *beauty* to sex can be a problem in human sex relations. Particularly for men, there are some misconceptions about beauty in the other sex. This is another example of popular notions about "sex appeal" that can be sadly misleading. If a woman is extremely beautiful, does that mean that she will be a superior or outstanding sexual partner?

The relationship between beauty (that is, in this context, sexual attractiveness) and sex (meaning sexual performance) has been commented upon by poets, philosophers, and novelists since time immemorial. Probably every man and woman has some assumptions about beauty (and/or handsomeness) and sex which influence their behavior in sexual relationships. What actually is the relationship between sexual *attractiveness* (or beauty) and sexual *performance*?

Many men have different preferences in what they desire in a sexually attractive woman (to them). We hear men on the street refer to themselves as "leg" men or "breast" men. The basic assumptions underlying many a man's looking at a woman from a sexual point of view is that a woman with a "sexy" figure will be more sexually satisfying and therefore a better sexual partner.

But the facts are that superior sexual performance does *not* necessarily go along with beauty. In fact, many very beautiful women have difficulty in their sexual functioning *because* they are so beautiful, that is, because of their reactions, and those of men, to their beauty.

One of the most beautiful women I ever had as a client in group therapy reported that she had slept around with lots of men but she never had had orgasm. She even denied that women had such a thing as an orgasm. Many men pursued this strikingly beautiful and attractive woman but evidently were disappointed in sexual relations with her. Her *attitude* toward sex were what interfered with her sexual performance and satisfaction despite her beautiful face and body.

In the same therapy group, another female client, a hauntingly beautiful black woman who had won several beauty contests with her voluptuous figure, stated that she never experienced an orgasm in intercourse either, despite considerable sexual experience. These two stunning women compared notes and later confronted me with questions about women having orgasms.

They both had all the necessary "standard equipment" and in addition were very beautiful in face and figure. They had lovely hair, flawless skin, and gorgeous figures, and yet they had never, as yet, been able to satisfy themselves nor their male partners in sexual relations. Their *assumptions* about themselves, men, and sex interfered with their adequate sexual performance. [But once again, assumptions and attitudes, if self-defeating, can be changed in psychotherapy.]

A common assumption among many men that beautiful women make better sexual partners can be broken down into specifics. The belief that because a woman has certain measurements that therefore she will perform better sexually is just one of those common notions that "ain't necessarily so." Likewise, a woman who assumes that merely because a man is handsome, he will therefore be a more adequate lover will often be sadly disappointed if she acts on this belief.

The fact that a man is tall, dark, and handsome really tells one very little about his sexual abilities in bed. In fact, many a handsome man, just because he is handsome, is so pursued by women that he may become very careless, thoughtless, and sloppy in his sexual performance. I have had many such good looking men in my private practice who thought they were great lovers; however, many women discovered that that was not the case.

Most people are *not* beautiful or handsome, and yet they have "standard equipment" as far as sexual capacity is concerned. *They therefore need not worry about their sexual performance merely because they are not "handsome" or "beautiful," as the case may be.* More important than beauty (or handsomeness), as far as sexual performance is concerned, is *attitude. And that you can change without ever looking in a mirror.*

Attitude is what makes the difference. The attractive woman sometimes assumes that all she has to do is just "be beautiful," whereas a plainer woman may go out of her way to be warm, responsive, and loving (much to her partner's delight). One's attitude toward sex is thus much more basic than any tape measurements or configurations or bone and flesh.

What can be said that is positive about the relationship between beauty and sex (since we have been saying some critical, negative things, so far)? Although different men seek different attributes of beauty in women, particularly the women they want for sexual partners, it would seem to be the case that a minimum of some kind of beauty (at least in the beholder's eyes) is necessary for some men. Otherwise they will not be attracted enough to respond sexually, that is, to have an erection. It certainly does help the sexual response of a man if a woman dresses attractively and pays attention to her hair and figure.

Cleanliness is also important to some people, both male and female (the counter-culture to the contrary notwithstanding). A certain minimum of cleanliness is helpful in making one sexually attractive to one's sexual partner.

Since "beauty" means different things to different people, as does sex for the that matter, the relationship of beauty and sex varies in each person. Therefore general conclusions having very wide application and are difficult to draw.

But perhaps we can say that beauty seems more critical to the human male (in order to have the minimum sexual response for sexual performance) and handsomeness is not as pressing a matter for many women. But attitudes toward sex are more basic and a better indicator of possible sexual performance than mere beauty.

Standards of beauty are largely culturally determined, it would seem. Each culture develops its own special set of values where sexual attractiveness is concerned. There are some authorities, however, who maintain that there are some universal standards of beauty that operate all over the world. Good-sized buttocks and breasts are frequently cited as perhaps universally approved standards of beauty. But we know that different men have different tastes in such matters. Perhaps a tentative conclusion might be that, with regard to feminine beauty, tastes are largely culturally determined. But in some respects ideas about beauty throughout the world do have much in common.

One fact is certain: in most regions of the world, men tend to place too great an emphasis on the more shallow or superficial physical aspects of womanly beauty. In this they delude themselves.

We need to get away from such shallow conceptions of beauty. These lead to self-defeating behavior in sexual relations. They frequently lead one up a blind alley because they are based upon false assumptions. Beauty obviously plays some part in sexual functioning, but *attitudes* would seem to be more basic than beauty.

SUGGESTED FURTHER READING

Ard, Ben N., Jr. "Worries About Breast Size," *Sexology,* 30 (1963), 117-119.

Ard, Ben N., Jr. "Worries About Penis Size," *Sexology,* 31 (1965), 697-699.

Ard, Ben N., Jr. "Do Beautiful Women Make Good Lovers?" *Sexology,* 33 (1967), 59-592.

Ard, Ben N., Jr. "How Important is Penis Size?" *Sexology,* 37 (1970), 19-21.

Ayalah, Daphna & Weinstock, Isaac J. *Breasts: Women Speak About Their Breasts and Their Lives.* New York: Summit Books, 1976.

Ellis, Albert, "The Beautification of Beauty," in Ellis, Albert. *The American Sexual Tragedy.* New York: Twayne, pp. 15-39.

Geis, H. Jon. "The Psychology of Dieting," *Rational Living,* 5 (1970), 24-33.

SUGGESTED FURTHER READING

"If you define urination or menstruation as dirty, then the human body becomes dirty through this semantic trickery... Redefining them with reality acceptance reduces the distance between what is and what ought to be."

Abraham H. Maslow

CHAPTER 3

MENSTRUATION AND MENOPAUSE:
WHAT MEN AND WOMEN HAD BETTER KNOW

Despite the fact that menstruation in most cases is a normal, natural process that occurs in all women (except in rather rare cases), many women seem to have some problems with menstruation which frequently are largely *psychological* in nature. This is not to discount the organic factors that can cause difficulties with menstruation but merely to emphasize that here we are primarily concerned with the psychological problems associated with menstruation.

By menstruation is meant the periodic discharge of bloody fluid from the uterus through the vagina, usually occurring during the period of a woman's sexual maturity, from puberty to the menopause (except when interrupted during pregnancy). This discharge normally occurs at approximately four-week intervals in most women, although the menstrual cycle may not be very regular in many women. The menstrual period is frequently said to start every twenty-eight days but it is subject to much variation from woman to woman and may vary in the same woman from month to month, depending on several factors.

Because lack of menstruation is a sign of pregnancy, any delay in the menstrual period may be, on occasion, cause of some alarm to a woman. But pregnancy is only one cause for the lack of menstruation. Even the fear of possible pregnancy may cause delay in the menstrual period, showing how psychological factors are very basic in such a normal biological function as menstruation. Sometimes marked delays or irregularities occur in women who have made long trips or moved to a different region with a somewhat different climate. Tension, worry, or radical wrenches in life patterns may cause delays in menstruation. And for some delays, despite investigation by the relevant professionals, there sometimes seems as if there is just no explanation available. This irregularity or fluctuation in periodicity is one of the basic reasons the so-called "safe period" or "rhythm method" of birth control is so unreliable: the supposedly "safe" period, when there is less likelihood of ovulation (and therefore conception), is not really safe because the supposed regular rhythm will have been thrown off by one or more of the many factors mentioned, such as physical illness, psychological stress, trips, change in climate, and so forth.

Menstruation usually begins in the early teens, although the actual age may vary considerably and still be within normal limits. Many problems have arisen in connection with menstruation because too many young girls have not been adequately prepared for the onset of menstruation *before* it actually occurs. I still continue to see women in my private practice who were not informed as to menstruation until *after* it occurred, if then. Needless to say, the sudden onset of such an unexpected phenomenon can be upsetting to a young girl, even though it is a perfectly natural event. But because education about menstruation is tied in with "sex education," many parents are evidently still hung up over the difficult task (for them) of imparting sane, sensible information about menstruation to their growing daughters.

Although there seems to be no known reason for a great deal of pain occurring around menstruation in the normal woman, it sometimes does occur. The more mild pain may be caused by the swelling of the uterus (resulting from the large amount of blood circulating through the walls), which leads to pressure on the nerves in the areas. Other factors which may make the pain more severe are such things as chronic constipation, incorrect balance of hormones, general poor health, or any abnormalities of structure of the ovaries, tubes, or uterus. Such matters should, of course, be discussed with a competent physician specializing in these areas. Sometimes birth control pills can give some relief from pain and other difficulties, although even such pills may not solve the problem entirely for all women. Sometimes the pain associated with menstruation is somewhat relieved after a woman has had her first pregnancy.

A rather common complaint among some teen-age girls (and some women beyond the teen years) is abdominal cramping just before or during menstruation. The organic reasons for this are not fully understood, but one factor may be the result of the congestion of blood in the pelvic region (perhaps due to progesterone withdrawal). Another possible explanation may be that uterine contractions, somewhat like those of early labor, may occur in some females.

Some authorities believe that various *psychological* factors influence the amount of pain a woman has during menstruation. If, after checking out the various possible organic factors with a physician, the woman suspects that psychological factors may be influencing her reactions to menstrual difficulties, she would be wise to check out any possible psychological factors with a competent psychologist.

There are many old wives' tales and superstitions centering around menstruation which may influence a woman's reactions to menstruation.

40

Such superstitions, since they are not founded on fact, cause some women unnecessary concern and needless worry. Some of these superstitions may be traced back to the Bible. A woman was thought to be "unclean" while menstruating, which meant that she was to be shunned as something harmful. It was thought (or rather assumed) that she could blight corn, make iron rust, and even cause madness in dogs. The menstrual fluid, by its odor, it was assumed, would cause fruit to fall from trees, destroy insects, and prevent seeds from growing. In some societies, because of these and other superstitions and false beliefs, females during menstruation were compelled to secret themselves and shun society. When people believe irrational things they act in irrational rather than rational ways. Some tribes even went so far as to punish with death any woman who failed to give due notice of being in that condition, so that she might be ostracized.

Women have been forbidden to enter church while menstruating (by decree of the Council of Niceae). If a man had intercourse with a woman while she was menstruating, according to Leviticus, then both of them were cut off from their people. Some people believed that bread would not rise, that beer would sour, and milk curdle if a menstruating woman had anything to do with them. It should hardly be necessary to say that all such notions are as erroneous as they are absurd. They are disproved every day by women who pay no attention to such claptrap and, in fact, conduct all of the operations mentioned very successfully, with none of the adverse reactions occurring.

Painful menstruation (dysmenorrhea) is something many women complain of from time to time. Some cultural factors may be operating here in some cases. Margaret Mead, the famous anthropologist, has said that

"Careful studies of dysmenorrhea in America have failed to reveal any consistent factors among women who manifest pain except exposure during childhood to another female who reported menstrual pain." (Mead, 1949, p.220)

Perhaps one of the ideas or assumptions about menstruation which most affects many people is the idea that intercourse is dangerous during a woman's monthly period. What are the relevant fact here? Some of these ideas about supposed "dangers" in having sexual intercourse during menstrual periods are simply a hangover from hearsay and superstition.

Are there any valid, scientific reasons for avoiding sexual intercourse during menstrual periods? Yes, there are some. There are two minor dangers, due to the fact that there are many bacteria in the vagina during the menstrual period. The bacteria grow in the menstrual discharge and produce a certain amount of odor. These bacteria can lead to infection of the male urethra, for one things. (This danger can be eliminated, of course, by wearing a condom over the penis during intercourse.) A second potential danger is that the movements of the penis in the vagina may force the bacteria into the uterus, which is possible at this time because the small mass of mucus which usually plugs the opening into the uterus is not there during menstruation. (A woman can insert a diaphragm to help avoid this latter possibility during intercourse, of course.)

What is a rational conclusion, then, regarding sexual intercourse during a woman's monthly period? For some women, it would seem to be less a matter of danger and more a matter of personal preference. Perhaps the urgency of sexual desire is a factor for some. This is, if a woman has a strong desire for sex during her period (which is sometimes the case for some women), and if there are no aesthetic objections on the part of either party involved, then there would seem to be no serious reason why sexual intercourse should *always* be avoided at this time, provided condoms and diaphragms are used. Some people, however, would simply prefer not to have intercourse during the menstrual period because of considerations of distaste, making sex less enjoyable for some at these times. Odors and messiness can be somewhat offset by strict attention to cleanliness through showers, douches, perfumes, deodorants, colognes, and so forth; but some people still might just prefer to have intercourse at a more mutually agreeable time.

Some women may find sexual intercourse during menstruation rather uncomfortable because of the menstrual blood and the sensitivity of the vaginal area at this time, especially during the first day or two, if there is a particularly heavy flow. Sometimes having sexual intercourse near the end of a woman's period may stir up her flow and thus cause some inconvenience. The possibilities for the man of urethritis or irritation of the penis have already been mentioned and should be considered. For these reasons, and due to the aesthetic preferences of the two people involved, couples may reasonably defer sexual intercourse during menstruation without subscribing to any of the irrational taboos forbidding such intercourse.

Some couples may usually not have sexual intercourse during menstruation, but on special occasions like anniversaries, birthdays, returns from long trips by a partner, or visits to special places, they may have intercourse even during menstruation because of the potency of the occasion, which seems to override other considerations. Such a flexible approach would seem to be a rational stance to take with regard to whether or not to have intercourse during menstruation. To each his own, within the above rational considerations, would seem a good motto in this regard.

Some women seem to be embarrassed about, or ashamed of, menstruation, as any professional in the field can testify. And yet, among the self-actualizing or psychologically healthy individuals studied by psychologist A.H. Maslow (1970, pp. 156-157), none of the women were embarrassed about, ashamed of, or felt ill at ease about any of the normal physiological processes such as menstruation, lactation, urination, defecation, birth, perspiration, body odors, and so forth. This attitude of acceptance of self and what is normal for being human would be a helpful attitude for every person to adopt.

Just as menstruation causes certain problems among some women, particularly where their irrational ideas, myths, assumptions, and taboos are concerned, problems sometimes arise for some women when menstruation ceases. The menopause, climacteric, or "change of life" refers to the irregular menstrual cycles which precede the stopping of ovulation and the regular monthly menstruation in women, which usually occurs sometime between their fortieth and fiftieth years, although there is variation here too, and is to be expected.

Too many women have too much unnecessary worry because of misunderstandings about the true nature of menopause and its consequences. Women need to know that menopause, like menstruation, is a normal event in the life of a woman and is not a catastrophe. Some women, in effect, make it a catastrophe by arbitrarily defining it as such.

What are the relevant, important facts about menopause? It usually starts with a decreasing amount of menstrual flow and an increasingly irregularity in the menstrual periods (in some women the periods even stop and then reappear several months later). This sort of thing of course makes it difficult to say just exactly when the menopause has started or been completed.

The hormonal changes in the production of the various endocrine glands have different side effects. The glands affect each other so that, when the ovaries cease to function as they have before, other glands are affected. Until the body achieves a new balance, some of the side effects of these endocrine imbalances reveal themselves in the characteristic symptoms of the menopause. The physical symptoms which are most commonly known, perhaps, are the "hot flashes" a woman may experience, due to the changes in the circulation of the blood. Usually the woman feels very warm, may look flushed, and perspire excessively. This situation may only last from a few seconds to a few minutes but is somewhat uncomfortable, even though normal. Some of the uncomfortable side effects of the menopause can be counteracted through hormone preparations. Some women think this is desirable even though it may prolong the process of menopause. Each woman should talk this matter over with her physician (gynecologist) before deciding what seems best for her as an individual.

At the time of the publication of this book, there would appear to be no clear-cut agreement among physicians as to whether or not women should be *routinely* placed on replacement therapy as the ovarian function declines in the menopause. Some physicians are the opinion that the majority of women require no treatment for menopause. Other physicians routinely prescribe the use of hormonal treatment to relieve menopausal symptoms. Prescribing oral contraceptive pills is one of the forms of treatment. Whichever path the woman decides to take, she can contribute a great deal to the menopause being a normal phenomenon in her family and her life by assuming an extra responsibility and making an extra effort to be pleasant, congenial, and noncritical, and particularly to suppress as best she can the mood changes which seem to occur for no apparent reason.

This latter approach derives from the possibility that some of the symptoms of the menopause may result from *psychological* as well as physiological factors. Many authorities in the field are of the opinion that some of the difficult times some women have during their menopause may be as much due to these *psychological* factors as to the organic conditions which may accompany it. That is, some of the reactions to menopause may be due more to *psychological* rather than merely organic factors. It may thus not be so much what happens to a woman during menopause as it may be what she says to herself (in effect, perhaps if not consciously) about her going through the menopause.

For example some of the false assumptions that may be found in some women's minds about menopause are that this change of life means, in effect, that their sex life is over and done with, so to speak; while others assume that it would not be "seemly" or "proper" for a woman past the menopause to continue an active sex life. Some assume they are *ipso facto* no longer attractive or desirable as a sexual partner. And so on. All these beliefs or unquestioned assumptions contribute to a very self-defeating attitude on the woman's part. Her behavior is prompted by these mistaken ideas and consequently she has a much more miserable time than would be necessary if she unlearned these irrational ideas.

One of the reasons for some of this mixed-up thinking about sex and the menopause is that too many people have simply identified "sex" with "reproduction" and therefore, when reproduction is no longer a possibility (after the menopause), they assume, mistakenly, that their sex life is at an end, or at least should be. But sex is obviously not merely for reproductive purposes; it is also a means for the expression of love and affection, companionship, and pleasure and enjoyment. Women who adopt this latter point of view frequently have better sex after their menopause than before. They have reported that they do not have to worry about getting pregnant anymore, and this is a real relief.

This identification of sex with reproduction, even though a false idea, is perhaps back of the unfortunate reactions some women have to hysterectomy, which is the surgical removal (total or partial) of the uterus. Since a hysterectomy thus means, in effect, the same thing so to speak as what the menopause means, that is, that the woman will not be able to have any more children, some women react to a hysterectomy in the same fashion as some women do the menopause. Here the same false assumptions are sometimes made about the hysterectomy meaning the end of a woman's sex life, with the self-defeating consequences as we previously saw applied to the implications about the menopause.

I have known clients who have had severe depressions after a hysterectomy. Some clients have assumed that no man would want them anymore after he found out that such an operation had been performed. This problem can be particularly difficult for a younger woman who has had a hysterectomy before she has had any children.

A woman needs to have her own worth as a person, and as a woman, more firmly based than upon the merely arbitrary definition of just being a baby factory. A woman had better think of herself as a worthwhile human being, just by virtue of being born, rather than only of value as a person who can have babies. Her *intrinsic* worth should never be in question (no matter how many or how few, if any, babies she may have); it should be her rock of Gibraltar, entirely secure and never to be threatened by any external considerations of her *extrinsic* worth (to others as a sexual partner, potential mother of children, or whatever).

A woman needs to continue to think of herself as a worthwhile person, whatever happens to her with regard to, menstruation or menopause. While women usually do have a uterus, and therefore the potential capacity to have babies, their worth and self-esteem or self-acceptance should never be based solely on that capacity. That is too narrow a definition of womanhood and, unfortunately, has been oversold to too many women.

The recent developments in women's liberation, while not always entirely rational, certainly should have made more women aware of the fact that they are much more than mere baby factories. Women are obviously entitled to equal status as human beings, as persons, regardless of whether or not they have any children whatsoever. Sex is much more than mere reproduction. Sex is indulged in much more often for reasons other than for mere reproduction of the species, which is the traditional idea which still causes so much trouble for too many women.

If women who are troubled with problems centering around menstruation and menopause will think through their basic philosophy of life and seriously examine their fundamental premises and assumptions, challenging and changing those which will not stand up to scientific scrutiny, and particularly questioning those ideas or assumptions which are

48

self-defeating, they can live more satisfying and enjoyable lives, even if they happen to have some problems with menstruation and/or menopause which can be resolved by getting the best scientific, philosophical and psychological help available.

SUGGESTED FURTHER READING

Brown, Fred, and Kempton, Rudolf T. *Sex Questions and Answers* (New York: McGraw-Hill, 2nd edition, 1970), Chapter 5, pp. 88-103.

Corner, George W., Jr. "Menstrual Cycle." *In* Ellis, Albert and Abarbanel, Albert (editors), *The Encyclopedia of Sexual Behavior* (New York: Hawthorn Books, 1961), volume 2, pp. 729-738.

Kelly, G. Lombard. "Menopause." *In* Ellis, Albert and Abarbanel, Albert (editors) *The Encyclopedia of Sexual Behavior* (New York: Hawthorn Books, 1961), volume 2, pp. 718-728.

Maslow, A. H. *Motivation and Personality* (New York: Harper & Row, 2nd ed., 1970)

Mead, Margaret. *Male and Female* (New York: Morrow, 1949).

Montague, Ashley. *Sex, Man & Society* (New York: Putnam, 1969), Chapter 13, pp. 109-119.

SUGGESTED FURTHER READING

"Masturbation is a normal physiological phenomenon. It is a form of sex-play which may be expected in most normal children, and which will normally disappear when mating occurs. Masturbation is so inferior to normal coitus in its capacity for affording sexual pleasure that no sensible person would resort to it except faute de mieux. Remove the difficulty of obtaining normal sexual intercourse, and no properly trained adult will care to practice masturbation. In any case, masturbation in itself is not harmful. The harm comes from...worrying about it. This worry is due to the widespread, but erroneous, teaching that the practice is wicked and harmful."

Bernard A. Bauer
Woman and Love
(Vol 2, 1927, p. xiii)

CHAPTER 4

MASTURBATION: A "SIN" OR A NATURAL, NORMAL PHENOMENON?

Masturbation, sometimes termed autoeroticism, probably amounts to one of the oldest or most perennial of sexual problems for human beings. It has been condemned and forbidden by religious moralists for so many years that even today, when we should know better, many people continue to worry and feel guilty about this perfectly normal, natural practice. By masturbation is meant any self-stimulation of the genitals, usually to the point of orgasm. Despite the growth of scientific knowledge about sex, even some so-called "professional" books have wrongly suggested that masturbation causes all sorts of troubles and illnesses, from pimples to insanity. Modern scientific knowledge has shown that these dire warnings are unjustified and that, in fact, masturbation will not hurt anyone.

However, many people still have problems with masturbation. Some little boys, unfortunately, are still threatened with: "If you don't stop that, I'll cut that thing off!" Too many little boys and girls are shamed unnecessarily for this perfectly natural and normal exploration and experimentation with their own bodies. It needs to be said, therefore, that masturbation will *not* "ruin you for life," as some people continue to think.

With the progress of sexology (the scientific study of sex), most of today's sex authorities admit that masturbation does not cause the harm people use to think it did. But there has developed a disguised, subtle, last-ditch stand against masturbation through vague warnings about "too much" of it, or masturbation "to excess." Even though most modern scientific books admit that masturbation is not the "danger" or "sin" it used to be considered (and still is today by some religious people), they still frequently end up with some such statement as: "It's all right *if not indulged to excess."*

But the person reading such statements nearly always jumps to the unwarranted conclusion that *his* masturbation is in excess, whatever that is. And we are thus right back where we started from with self-sabotaging, self-defeating guilt feelings over what is a perfectly normal, natural act. Nobody ever spells out how much masturbation is "too much."

The so-called "modern" approach that many parents are advised to follow is to divert or distract the child when he plays with his genitals. But when he makes noises with his lips (bubbling them with his fingers) or plays with his fingers or toes we don't hand him a toy or plaything. Thus we in effect teach him that touching his genitals in somehow had and wrong. This is the beginning of the guilt feelings which sometimes afflict people for the rest of their lives.

From the physical point of view, the fear of "excessive" masturbation is simply unjustified, because the body has a natural, built-in means of preventing any such excess. Tumescence, or the filling of the blood vessels of the genital organs, is necessary for masturbation, and when a person's physiological limits are approached, tumescence simply does not occur. When a boy has masturbated several times, let us say, and reaches whatever happens to be his particular physiological limit, his penis just refuses to respond any further - he simply doesn't get an erection anymore for a while (for what is called a refractory period). While a girl obviously does not have an erection like a boy, tumescence will not occur in her genital organs either after she has reached her physiological limit, which varies from individual to individual.

This persistent worry about masturbation "to excess" probably indicates on the part of some so-called authorities a continued basic objection to masturbation in and of itself. It can be traced back in our culture to a long-standing hostile view of sex in general. This comes from the traditional religious appraisals which have been the major influence upon sex values and attitudes in this culture. (Ard, *Rational Sex Ethics*, 1989)

According to the most conservative religious leaders, the only form of acceptable sexual behavior is sexual intercourse with one's spouse. Any kind of sex other than intercourse within a lifelong, monogamous marriage is condemned.

Heterosexual behavior before marriage, particularly, is most strenuously objected to from the conventional religious point of view. This being so, the major alternatives open to young people are homosexuality and masturbation.

Perhaps only a relatively few people become involved with homosexuality because of the intense condemnation of premarital intercourse, although the number may be considerably greater than most people realize. Still, many turn to masturbation for sexual relief in our culture, especially in the early years before marriage. And yet the lingering objection to sex, expressed in the warnings of the supposed dangers of "excessive" masturbation, cruelly afflicts too many people with unnecessary guilt and worry.

If a person is not supposed to indulge in premarital intercourse, then masturbation would seem to provide a temporarily satisfactory outlet for his or her sexual drives. The old view fostered in our Judeo-Christian culture by religious leaders that complete abstinence should be followed before marriage is simply unrealistic in view of what we now know about human sexuality.

What is a person to do who has guilt feelings about his or her masturbation? First of all, it would be better if he could dismiss all such irrational ideas about masturbation. A person had better vigorously challenge, attack, and get rid of all such unreasonable, self-defeating ideas, and accept the practice as a natural phenomenon, a normal outlet for sexual desires when sexual intercourse is not available. If the person has long-standing deep-seated feelings of guilt, he or she had better seek professional help in working through the ideas causing such feelings and eliminating them. (Ard, *Living Without Guilt and/or Blame: Conscience, Superego and Psychotherapy,* 1983)

One young divorcee whose husband had left her began masturbating when her sexual satisfaction was no longer available. When she came to see me as a client, she felt so guilty about her masturbation that she could not even say the word, even though she had come to counseling sessions to get help with her problem of masturbation.

I had to, in effect, play something akin to "Twenty Questions" with her, since she could not talk about her problem at first. I asked her, after much silence and struggling on her part, if she would like for me to ask her some questions to get her started. She nodded yes.

Since she seemed so embarrassed and guilty, sitting with her head down so that I hardly saw more than the top of her head, I asked her if she had done something which she felt guilty about. She nodded yes. I asked her if it was something she had done with someone else. She shook her head no. Naturally, I then asked her if it was something she had done alone. She nodded yes. By this process of question asking and deduction, I was finally able to inquire if her problem was masturbation. She nodded yes.

This young woman, in her twenties and divorced, had a young daughter. She had been concerned about this problem because she had noticed that her daughter had been masturbating. She was afraid that, as a mother who had not resolved her own problem with masturbation, she might be responsible for her daughter's having serious trouble with masturbation.

Once I was able to say the dreaded word, it seemed to open things up and her whole story spilled out, with tears as an accompaniment. Once I told her that others had similar fears and guilt feelings and had been able to work them through, she hesitantly began to talk about her feelings regarding masturbation.

As a young child, she said, she had masturbated (as many children- perhaps most - do). Usually she masturbated under the covers after she thought her parents had left her alone for the night. However, on one occasion, which she remembered vividly, her parents were giving a dinner party. The mother and father and their invited guests were able to sneak into her bedroom unnoticed while the lights were out. Suddenly, they snapped on the lights, pulled back the covers, and all laughed uproariously at this little girl, caught in the act of masturbating.

The insensitivity of these adults is hard to believe. Yet, it illustrates to what lengths some parents and other elders may go in an effort to humiliate and shame children when the latter express their natural, normal sexual drives. The fact that these adults were so amused shows a grotesque unconcern for the privacy and feelings of this young girl. The parents had also taken this young girl to a physician and shamed her again by asking him to make her stop masturbating.

Not surprisingly, she came to feel that the act of masturbation was a terrible thing, an evil, dirty, sinful, animallike habit which was so horrible that even then, as an adult with a child of her own, she could not even say the word. She believed masturbation was a terrible thing because of what she had learned from her parents.

When asked why she thought it was such a terrible thing, this young woman could only repeat what she had heard as a child: that masturbation was wrong and a sign of depravity. When asked what she thought about when she heard the word masturbation, she said she thought about dogs rubbing up against various objects.

I suggested to her that she had better stop repeating to herself (or reindoctrinating herself with) all the nonsense her parents had fed her. I told her that masturbation was a normal, natural thing for any person, and especially for one who had just been separated from her husband. I recommended some books about masturbation and sex in general so that she could check out what I was telling her and not believe it merely because I had said that it was so.

Thus she began to root out the old beliefs which had never been questioned and which had caused her needless suffering. It was not the masturbation itself which was causing her all the trouble, but rather the gnawing (but irrational) *belief* in the back of her mind that she was hardly fit to live because she masturbated.

As she began to weed out these self-defeating beliefs, her feelings about herself began to improve and she began to get better. Changing one's early values, particularly about sex, is not an easy task. But it can be done - and it is sometimes a necessary task to be accomplished, difficult though it may be.

Too many people, for too many years, have assumed without question that masturbation is bad, unclean, sinful, and unhealthy. When young people are taught these sorts of things, they grow up feeling guilty whenever they have a sexual impulse or thought. This can create havoc in a marriage and unhappiness for the person living alone.

I predicted to this young lady that, after a few years had passed and she had possibly remarried, she and her new husband would look back on these trying times for her and actually laugh. She thought, at the time, that this suggestion was a bit farfetched, to say the least.

But after much hard work on her part (involving homework and bibliotherapy), coupled with much reading and re-thinking about what values she wanted to subscribe to, both for herself and her growing young daughter, she was able to come into my office and say sincerely that she believed masturbation was natural, acceptable form of sexual release. When she was able to say this and mean it, she was indeed well on the way to recovery.

She had learned that it was quite reasonable for a young woman to masturbate if she had been married and accustomed to regular intercourse, and then suddenly did not have husband around to provide that sexual satisfaction. It was not at all shameful for such a woman to return to a former means of satisfying her normal sexual desires, namely, masturbation.

When she accepted this as natural and normal, she was cured. She finally learned to accept herself as a normal woman, with all the sexual desires to be expected in a normally functioning woman.

She resumed dating and later married again. Several years afterward, she sent me a Christmas card from another state with some comments added that indicated that she had, indeed, been cured of her previous sexual problem. She wrote:

> Dear Dr. Ard:
>
> You will never believe what has happened to me and my new husband. We were sitting here before the fireplace talking and I began to make a few guarded remarks about masturbation, usually couched in third person terms of "people" and what "they" do regarding masturbation. My husband, in a very relaxed manner, laughed and said that he has masturbated, hadn't I?
>
> Soon I was using "you" and "I" in our conversation about masturbation. It was such a relief! We could laugh and look back on my previous overconcern about masturbation and put it in the proper perspective. And I remembered something you had said years before about something like this happening. I never thought it would happen at that time, but you were right, it did happen. Many thanks.
>
> P. S. Just thought you would like to know.

Indeed I was glad to hear that she had continued to consolidate the gains she had made in the psychotherapy sessions we had had years before and that her newfound position regarding masturbation had served her much better than her previous indoctrination in conventional morality.

So we see that, no matter to what great lengths society and parents may go to teach youngsters that sex and masturbation are sinful and evil, such irrational ideas can be rooted out, questioned and replaced by less self-defeating and more rational ones.

Thus it is possible to get rid of long-standing guilt feelings about masturbation. (Ard, 1983, 1989) The essence of the problem is that one had better get rid of the self-damaging thoughts surrounding sex and masturbation: that is, to challenge and change the assumptions about it, particularly the notion that in our children and in ourselves it is in any way harmful or bad. One had better accept masturbation as perfectly normal, natural part of life.

Masturbation generally causes problems in people's lives at various stages. Typically, parents are concerned about the practice in young children when the latter first discover their genitals. This is in fact largely exploration, but can be the start of problems, particularly if the parents slap the child's hand or tie his arms down at night.

Masturbation probably causes people the most trouble during adolescence, when the incidence and frequency are probably greatest. Nearly all boys masturbate during adolescence and many girls as well, although the incidence among girls is not as high as among boys. This is probably due to the influence of conventional culture upon girls; that is, the culture is much stricter with regard to girls and any and all sexual behavior than it is with boys.

Masturbation may cease to be much of a problem when heterosexual intercourse becomes more readily available. In fact, the French have a phrase which is applied to masturbation: it is said to occur *faute de mieux* (or for lack of something better). Sexual intercourse is so much more satisfying than masturbation that, when the former is available, most people will choose that over the latter.

But at various times in later life, after adulthood and marriage, some people have problems with masturbation again because of misunderstandings and false assumptions about sex, and masturbation in particular. During long absences from one's spouse, an individual may turn to self-gratification. During long sicknesses and sometimes during a pregnancy some couples may resort to the practice. Even where health poses no problems, some individuals may turn to masturbation rather than bother a spouse who desires sex less frequently. All of these uses of the act are legitimate and should cause no problems, except where individuals still cling to the mistaken notion that masturbation is somehow wrong, sinful or bad. If one can accept the fact that masturbation is a natural, normal phenomenon and a legitimate outlet for sexual desire, than most of the problems mentioned can be resolved.

Some clients of mine have reacted negatively when I have suggested that they follow some of the Masters and Johnson techniques of stimulation of their partner's erogenous zones. Many label all such activity simply as "masturbation." When I have suggested to clients that the husband might try to bring his wife to orgasm manually on occasion, some of them respond negatively and refuse to try this bit of behavior, simply because they cannot bring themselves to condone what they consider "masturbation." When I have suggested that some wives might wish to use a vibrator to stimulate themselves in order to learn about their orgasmic response (if they are having difficulties with orgasm), once again they sometimes cannot let themselves even touch their bodies "down there" in any way which might even remotely be considered in their minds as "masturbation."

So we see to what lengths some people go to avoid masturbation and still have difficulty with it. What is really needed is much more sex education for adults as well as for young people, so that everyone learns that masturbation is not a terrible thing, that it is not dirty, evil, or sinful.

Changing one's irrational assumptions as to masturbation and sex in general is one way to sexual sanity. Despite all the progress that has been made in sexology, some people still have reservations about masturbation. Insofar as these reservations are irrational, they had better be eradicated and eliminated.

Little girls need to learn about masturbation from adults who have a healthy attitude toward sex, rather than learning masturbatory techniques from peers who may tell them many falsehoods about sex. Some little girls or adolescent ones masturbate with objects that are dangerous, such as bottles, pencils, hairpins, and so on. No object that could be harmful should be inserted into the vagina. Surgeons have removed an unbelievable array of makeshift phallic objects from young girls and young women that have masturbated with such harmful implements out of ignorance.

Some people are shocked when any suggestion is made that we had better teach young women how to masturbate in a healthy fashion. Since they are probably going to masturbate anyway, any rational consideration of the problem would seem to indicate such a course of action was indicated, if we really want to help young people integrate sex in their lives in a healthy way.

The problem is not as pressing for boys, since they tend to masturbate with their hand or at least do not need to insert any foreign objects to attain sexual satisfaction. But girls are sometimes likely to turn to a variety of harmful objects if they are not forewarned against them.

While in this book I have not given much space to tables of research findings (since statistics tend to turn a lot of people off), one bit of research should perhaps be mentioned about masturbation. Women who have masturbated to the point of orgasm before marriage have been found to be more likely to have orgasm through intercourse in marriage. Thus we have further reason for educating people as to masturbation.

SUGGESTED FURTHER READING

Ard, Ben J., Jr. "Needless Worry About Masturbation," *Sexology*,
31 (1964), 46-48.

Ard, Ben N., Jr. "Masturbation Caused Her Torment," *Sexology*,
34 (1968), 807-809.

Ard, Ben N., Jr. *Living Without Guilt and/or Blame: Conscience, Superego
and Psychotherapy.* Smithtown, N.J.: Exposition Press, 1983.

Ard, Ben Neal, Jr. *Rational Sex Ethics.* New York: Peter Lang,
2nd edition, 1989.

Dearborn, Lester W. "Masturbation," *in* Fishbein, Morris & Burgess, Ernest
(Editors) *Successful Marriage.* Marriage Garden City, N.Y.:
Doubleday, 1963, pp. 350-361.

Ellis, Albert. "The Art and Science of Masturbation," *in* Ellis, Albert,
Sex and the Liberated Man. Secaucus, N.J.: Lyle Stuart, 1976,
pp. 38-67.

Harper, Robert A. & Stokes, Walter. "Masturbation," pp. 11-16, "A Guide
for Parents on the Masturbation of Children," pp. 17-21, *in*
Harper, Robert A. & Stockes, Walter. *45 Levels to Sexual*

66

Understanding and Enjoyment. Englewood Clifs, N.J.: Prentice-
Hall, 1971.

Johnson, Warren R. "Masturbation," pp. 319-326 *in* Broderick, Carlfred B.
& Bernard, Jessie (Editors) *The Individual, Sex, & Society.*
Baltimore: Johns Hopkins, 1969.

Katchadourian, Herant A. & Lunde, Donald T. "Autoeroticism," pp. 259-284,
in Katchadourian, Herant A. & Lunder, Donald T. *Fundamentals of
Human Sexuality.* New York: Holt, Rinehart & Winston, 2nd
edition, 1975.

Pomeroy, Wardell B. "Masturbation," pp. 125-133, *in* Pomeroy, Wardell B.
Sex & Girls. New York: Delacorte Press, 1969.

"Unmarried adults are approaching sex as a fact rather than a theory. They are accepting their sexual organization frankly as an instrument for personal growth and emotional completion with social stabilization, rather than hypocritically as a function designed by divine plan only for the procreation of pure beings whose excuse for living was that they might die in purity to attain happiness in a world to come. They appreciate that sex is the source of life, but believe that a sexless life in a mockery after biologic maturation, because it is contrary to nature."

Ira S. Wile
The Sex Life of the Unmarried Adult
(1934, p. 52)

CHAPTER 5

PREMARITAL SEX: THE "FIRST SIN" OR
THE WAVE OF THE FUTURE?

Another of the perennial sexual problems facing many people is whether or not to have premarital sex. Perhaps some people's view that premarital sex is *the* primary sexual issue facing every individual relates to the assumption that sexual problems are supposedly solved once a couple are married; at least they then have a legitimate outlet for sex for the first time in their lives, from the conventional point of view.

According to the customary view in our culture, premarital sex is forbidden because the only legitimate outlet for sex is assumed to be within marriage. In this culture, such conventional views are derived from the traditional Judeo-Christian religious code. While this view still represents the code to which the most lip service is given in public, times are changing fast and particularly with regard to attitudes toward premarital sex. Therefore, many people are faced with a dilemma with regard to attitudes toward premarital sex. To swing or not to swing, that is the question for many an individual these days.

Part of the problem of premarital sex would seem to arise out of the confusion of sex with *reproduction*; the two are not synonymous. But too often in the past, people of conservative beliefs have just assumed that sex meant reproduction and that was its primary if not basic purpose. The fact that sex serves other purposes was not openly acknowledged very often.

One young woman who was a client of mine may perhaps illustrate this confusion of sex with reproduction and show how this traditional view can cause problems. This young woman was a graduate student in a large western university. While she was describing her family background to me she touched on her sex education. She said her mother had carefully explained "all about sex" to her when my client was a rather young girl; her mother was clear about where babies come from and how they got there in the first place. In other words, this mother gave this daughter an "excellent" sex education, if sex is thought of only as reproduction.

My client said, by way of summary, that she assumed if one wanted a child one would look for a good mate, marry him, perform the sex act with him, wait nine months, and then one would have the child one wanted. Later on, as one wanted more children, one would have sexual intercourse again, once for each child one wanted, basically. So, according to this view of sex, one might have sex several times during a marriage, depending upon how many children one wanted. It was as simply as that! This young lady said she had this understanding as a quite young child and, with this understanding, had difficulty seeing why adults seemed to have so much trouble with sex, as they obviously appeared to her to have.

My client reported that it was not until she passed puberty and began to date and have sexual desires that she began to realize that her mother had not told her the whole story about sex. It was because people had sexual desires which were entirely unrelated to any desire for children that sex was a problem for adults. Sex, she discovered, was not merely a matter of reproduction but more basically a matter of sexual desires, coupled with desires for affection, touching, companionship, orgasm and pleasure and enjoyment. In other words, sex was fun! Her mother, like so many mothers (as well as many fathers), when faced with the task of sex education, assumed she had done her duty when she had completed an explanation of the reproductive phase. This identification of sex with reproduction is a logical mistake because it obviously overlooks the fact that human beings have sexual relations many, many times during a lifetime and yet the reproductive results occur only in a minute minority of the instances of sexual intercourse. People have sexual intercourse for the purpose of having children only on a very few occasions during their lifetime. But they make love (hopefully) many, many more times than they have children.

This young woman, who was a client of mine while I was a psychologist on a university campus, discovered that she could not be completely honest about sex even with her girl friends in the dormitory. She was rethinking her philosophy of life, including her attitudes toward sex, and particularly regarding premarital sex (a not uncommon occurrence among college students). She could talk over the pros and cons in confidence with me but when she tried to discuss such matters with the young women in the dormitory, she was ostracized merely because she said there might be come occasions when she felt that premarital sex was justified; that is, there might be certain situations in which she would consider premarital sex in a positive light. For those who assume without question that any premarital sex is a sin or amounts to "promiscuity," practically by definition, any such discussion of conditions under which premarital sex would be appropriately acceptable is unthinkable. So the young women in the dormitory labelled this young client of mine as a "bad" young woman and ostracized her thereafter.

Our culture has been particularly hard on young women with regard to sex in general. For many years young women are reared to think of premarital sex as bad and therefore to keep the young men at arm's length. Parents sometimes advise daughters not to let the young men touch them. After twenty years, approximately, of keeping the boys at arm's length, when a young woman marries, she is expected to drop all of her inhibitions, hesitations, reticence, and modesty and overnight (practically as she drops her wedding veil) become a warmly loving, passionate sexual partner. Some have even defined the "ideal" as one who is a perfect lady in the drawing room, a gourmet cook in the kitchen, and a "hussy" in the bedroom. That's asking a bit much, it would seem, particularly when we are willing to at least educate the young woman to be a good cook, to entertain, and so on. Evidently many people are not willing to learn how to be good in bed. No one asks, "How are you in bed?" In fact, the common assumption in our culture is that one need not learn about sex; one merely "does what comes naturally." And yet the facts are that one learns to make love just as well as one learns to cook and put on a dinner party.

Many people assume that sex is instinctual and that, therefore, there is no need to teach anyone anything much about it. Sex is instinctual among the lower animals but, as one ascends the phylogenetic scale from the lower animals such as rats through chimpanzees to man, instinct plays less and less a part in the sexual behavior of the various species. In rats, instinct dictates such behavior, but by the time one gets to chimpanzees learning enters in more. And by the time one gets to humans, *learning* is largely what explains their sexual behavior. Humans do have a sexual drive but it is not as specific as instincts in the lower animals.

Attitudes are much more important in humans and explain a lot of otherwise inexplicable human behavior. The *value premises* that humans operate on determine a lot of their behavior in the sexual area.

Perhaps another case may illustrate the importance of values, premises, and attitudes in the sexual behavior of humans. Men as well as women have their problems with regard to premarital sex. One young man who was a client of mine may illustrate how confused and mixed up people in our culture can become over premarital sex. This young man loudly and insistently proclaimed that he intended, at all costs, to marry a virgin. Yet he spent most of his time eliminating all the young women he could from that category. He loved the "chase" and would pursue a young woman for many months if she resisted his advances. But the minute any woman succumbed to his sexual overtures and went to bed with him, he immediately dropped her. He assumed that she was "no good" if she was willing to have premarital sex, and therefore he had eliminated another woman from the category of a possible mate for him. Many men in our culture have these irrational attitudes toward premarital sex. Such ideas, as this young man's illustrate, are obviously very contradictory, but because he was able to compartmentalize his thinking he continued this pattern of being a "stud" with the ladies, never able to find a "nice" girl to marry.

This young man happened to belong to a church where he would go and confess his sins (of having premarital sex) on a Sunday and then promptly proceed to pursue the ladies through the rest of the week (frequently very successfully), then repeat the whole process again and again. He did not realize that his behavior was self-defeating or contradictory. He thought he was merely doing what comes naturally and what all the boys would like to do. He was just more successful than others. He thought he was having a ball and could not see anything wrong in his pattern of life. But he did wonder, occasionally, why he was unable to find a "nice" girl (one who would not have premarital sex with him), one who would make him a good wife. He assumed that all women were tramps because they went to bed with him so readily. He felt that *they* were immoral! It never occurred to him that his behavior was unethical at all. He assumed (along with so many men in our culture) that it was the man's role to try to get all that he could sexually and that it was strictly up to the woman to set the limits. The man, according to this view, is to push the limits at all times, using whatever means he wishes (liquor, talk of love, promises of marriage, etc.) to obtain premarital sex, while it is up to the woman to say no. The premarital sex game thus turns out, frequently, to be a "wrestling match." The old saw that some men use may be mentioned here as a typical ploy: "Let's go out and let my conscience by your guide."

Women are taught and urged to be sexually attractive but not sexually active. Thus we have women trained to be sexual *teasers* but not sexual *satisfiers*. The premarital sex game, under these conditions, can hardly be satisfying to either sex. These conditions tend to make women slightly paranoid about men's sexual intentions, that is, to assume that all men are dirty dogs who are always out to love 'em and leave 'em. These conditions tend to make many men assume that all women are simply out to trap them into marriage by hook or crook. Thus the "war between the sexes" continues, with little hope for the future, so long as many people continue to assume without question the conventional attitudes toward sex. (Ard, *Rational Sex Ethics*, 1989) Our language even helps perpetuate part of the problem by constantly referring to the opposite sex rather than the *other* sex. Hopefully, in the future, rather than the sexes constantly being in opposition to each other, they can look to the other sex for cooperation, compassion, pleasure and enjoyment.

The problems revolving around premarital sex are faced in a variety of ways by different people. Even when some individuals resolve not to have any premarital sex, the problems are not all eliminated. Consider the quandary of the virginal male. (Cf. Glassberg, 1970) Despite much talk and writing about the "sexual revolution," wherein more people are assumed to be not as virginal as once used to be the case, there continue to be males who are bothered by the fact that they are virginal long past the time when most males are not. In my private practice as a psychologist, marriage counselor and sex therapist I continue to see some male clients with this problem.

Some authorities still believe that for an unknown percentage of males virginity is the only acceptable pattern. Many moral authorities would still hold forth for virginity for both male and females. That some males believe this is obviously a fact, and that such males have a "right" to their stand on virginity is also true, in one sense, aside from the question of whether or not such a position is a wise and reasonable one to take.

Some men's self-image and self-respect seem to hinge upon whether or not women think they are "manly" or not. If a woman scoffs at a man's virility, he may panic if he doubts his ability to perform the sexual act, or if he is in fact trying to remain a virgin. Some authorities maintain that a man must be unreservedly accepted and approved by those who share in any affectional association. However, such an assumption may be at the core of the quandary of the virginal male. In the case where a woman scoffs at a man who will not go to bed with her, his notion that he must have her approval may be said to have caused his panic reaction. The woman in the situation has failed to "unreservedly" provide this so direly needed approval. Perhaps the man, along with many others in our culture, had better reevaluate his philosophic assumptions (or value premises, or conscience, or unquestioned superego presumptions) and henceforth not be threatened when a significant other does not unreservedly approve of him.

If he did a thorough job of reexamining his basic philosophical assumptions (about himself, others, and sex), he would henceforth not be unnecessarily bothered by rejection (or the fear of possible rejection) by women, or the failure to live up to any expectations, including those of his father, his conscience or superego, or anyone else. (Ard, 1983)

Many males in our culture remain virginal because of their irrational fear of possible rejection, or fear of failure in their performance in the sexual area. It is their fear of failure and possible rejection that can be forthrightly attacked and overcome through discussions of basic values and "homework assignments," wherein the client finds out that he can overcome these fears. It is a difficult task in psychotherapy, but not impossible. He can find out that he fairly assuredly has "standard equipment" and can function adequately as a male, provided he does not seek perfection and demand constant approval from others.

Some virginal males arbitrarily define any premarital sex as "sin" or "promiscuity" and therefore remain virginal because they assume without questioning it that the worst thing they could possibly do is get some woman pregnant before marriage. Sometimes they even assume that to make any sexual overture to a woman is to be too "aggressive" and even "animallike." They may have been taught these ideas by their mothers.

Such a virginal male had better revise his viewpoint and come to see sex as a good, normal, natural part of life. Sex is enjoyable, it can even be fun. It becomes self-defeating when feared or when one's fear of failure to perform perfectly is not questioned and reduced, if not eliminated entirely. Additional concepts of "purity" might better be examined and challenged, as well as the traditional, conventional superego assumptions that any premarital sex is, by arbitrary definition, promiscuity or a sin.

The question is often raised in such cases, should the clinician be concerned with the individual's effort to achieve self-actualizing maturity *according to his (the client's) own convictions and standards?* Is the proper function of the clinician that of reinforcing the values of the individual so that he may maintain and increase the quality of his (the client's) own self-image? The crucial issue here is whether the client's own convictions, standards and values are self-defeating or not. If they are, they had better be reexamined, challenged and changed. *Always* following one's own conscience or superego demands is *not* the answer. The consequences had better be examined, and if they are detrimental they can be changed so as to enable the client to live a better, fuller life. (Ard, 1983)

A client cannot live a satisfactory, full life and continue to be threatened by anyone who questions his virility. He can learn to question any assumption that he has that his *intrinsic* worthwhileness as a person depends upon his sexual performance (as contrasted with *extrinsic* evaluations by others). The client's own "self-determined norm" may be wise or unwise, satisfying or self-defeating, in its consequences. And because a client's norms are rarely questioned, *either by the client or the clinician,* we continue to have clients with problems like those of the virginal male.

When clinicians and clients can begin to examine the consequences for the client of acting on unquestioned assumptions about the latter's worthwhileness as a person, his maleness, his masculinity, his virility, and the approval of significant others, as well as the supposed sinfulness of sex, then both client and clinician can work together to make improvements in the client's thinking and life, and thereby help his future become more satisfying by integrating sex in his life in a more psychologically mature fashion.

The quandary of the virginal male has been presented first, since the more usual discussion is of the virginal female. But the above considerations would serve just as well with the latter. Many women (despite the sexual revolution, or sexual renaissance) in our culture still have a great deal of trouble with the question of whether or not to have premarital sex. This continues to be so, despite all the talk about the sexual renaissance or the sexual revolution.

One of the questions still in many a woman's mind today is whether or not a man will continue to *respect* her if she has premarital intercourse with him. As we have seen from the case of the man who wanted to marry a virgin, this point is not entirely unfounded. Some men will lose respect for women they have premarital intercourse with, if the men hold to the traditional double standard which says, in effect, that it is all right for men to have premarital intercourse but it is not all right for "nice" or "good" women to do the same.

The very statement of the double standard should make fairly obvious its faults as a guide to rational sex ethics. (Ard, 1989) The double standard assumed that there are only two kinds of women: the nice kind that are virgins before marriage (and who therefore are the kind men want to marry) and the not-so-nice kind that men are free to play around with before marriage (and whom they frequently avidly pursue). The facts of the case are, however, that there are not merely two kinds of women, the good and the bad, but actually many, many variations.

One client of mine may perhaps illustrate the absurd lengths to which some humans beings go in this matter of premarital sex. This young woman was a nurse and had considerable experience in premarital sex with a variety of men. She was Jewish but dated men from a variety of backgrounds. One day a young Jewish doctor came to town and began dating her. She set her cap for him, as the saying goes. She wanted to marry him. He fell in love with her and hotly pursued her, protesting his love for her and trying to persuade her to have premarital intercourse with him. He told her he wanted to marry her. She felt strong sexual desire for him but admitted confidentially that if she went to bed with him she was afraid he would never marry her. So she refused him the sexual favors she had granted to men she cared less for, whom in fact she did not love. He went along with her stand of no premarital sex, assuming that she was a "nice" girl and was only doing what was "proper." However, one day he discovered that she had in fact been sleeping around with a number of men in town (such matters are sometimes hard to cover up forever), and he blew his stack.

When he confronted her with the facts she had to admit that it was true that she had slept with men she did not love and was still refusing him the sexual expression of the deep love she said she had for him (which she seemed in fact to have). Such is the absurd length to which some women are pushed in their confused thinking about whether or not to have premarital sex.

Another case illustration may show how virginal young women even in this modern age attempt to resolve their dilemmas about premarital sex. I had another client who was a college student at a Midwestern university where I was the psychologist in the student health service. She had been taught in the usual conventional manner that the worst thing she could possibly do with a young man was to have premarital intercourse. So much stress was put on this "penis in the vagina" as the worst of all possible sins that she believed the dictum unquestioningly. Otherwise, she was a most modern young lady and believed that it was all right to do everything else that one could possibly think of with a young man that she was in love with, and she proceeded to do just that. She is what is known as a "technical virgin" or "demi-virgin," in that she had gone to a motel with a young man, spent the night, taken off all her clothes, and performed all the imaginable kinds of sexual foreplay, but they were very careful never to have the penis enter the vagina. So, technically speaking, she was still a virgin. But if this sort of behavior is not patently absurd, it comes about as close as it is possible to come to self-defeating, mixed-up thinking and behavior.

We Americans, particularly of the conventional variety, have made such a big thing out of premarital sex as the worst of all possible things that young people who do not think through the implications of the traditional views come out with such absurd behavior as "anything goes" as long as the penis does not enter the vagina. Some plain premarital intercourse (with proper precautions being taken) would seem healthier to most people who have not swallowed whole the traditional, conventional views about sex which are still prevalent in our culture.

Another example of a very common attitude these days with regard to premarital sex is the point of view of quite a few women in our culture, namely that premarital intercourse is all right *if one is in love* (and presumably contemplating marriage). And yet, this sometimes proves a farce also. I have had young women on university campuses report to me that they followed the rule, "no love, no sex," and yet also reported they had been "in love" with fifty or sixty young men during the course of the past academic year! One wonders if the "love" bit was not merely an excuse for having premarital sex. Much more honesty is needed in premarital sexual relations, including self-honesty.

In previous days, before birth control methods reached their present state of advancement, the fear of pregnancy kept some people from having premarital sex. Venereal disease, or the fear of VD, also kept some from premarital sex. But now in these days of "the pill" and modern medicine, when the cure for VD (short of herpes and AIDS) is possible, things are changing and those old scare techniques are insufficient with modern people who know the facts.

Fear of loss of one's good reputation kept others from indulging in premarital sex. While this loss of "reputation" can still be a problem to some women in certain circles (in parts of the South, the Midwest, the Bible Belts, small towns, rural areas, and conservative communities), changing attitudes toward premarital sex seem to be spreading throughout many part of the United States. (Reiss, 1960, 1967)

So ultimately the problem of premarital sex reduces to what one's basic attitude toward sex is. (Ard, 1989) If one arbitrarily defines sex as a bad thing outside of marriage, that is, a sin), then one may indeed have a problem. If one thinks of sex as a normal, natural, good part of life, when handled with reason, discretion, and responsibility, then premarital sex can be integrated into a good life, despite the fact that many people in our culture continue to have many irrational ideas and assumptions about premarital sex.

If sex is a normal drive in human beings, and the consequences of premarital sexual intercourse are adequately prepared for, then it would seem that premarital sex could be integrated in a responsible fashion in a person's life, despite the fact that many people in our culture still continue to label any and all premarital sex as a sin, or at least promiscuity or exploitation, by arbitrary definition.

SUGGESTED FURTHER READING

Ard, Ben N., Jr. "Commentary on the Quandary of a Virginal Male," *The Family Coordinator*, 19 (1970), 86-87.

Ard, Ben N., Jr. *Living Without Guilt and/or Blame: Conscience, Superego and Psychotherapy.* Smithtown, New York: Exposition Press, 1983.

Ard, Ben Neal, Jr. *Rational Sex Ethics.* New York: Peter Lang, 1989.

Bell, Robert R. *Premarital Sex in a Changing Society.* Englewood Cliffs, N.J.: Prentice Hall, 1966.

Ehrmann, Winston. *Premarital Dating Behavior.* New York: Henry Holt, 1959.

Ellis, Albert. "On Premarital Sex Relations," *in* Albert Ellis. *Sex Without Guilt.* New York: Lyle Stuart, 1958, pp. 33-50.

Glassberg, Bert Y. "The Quandary of a Virginal Male," *The Family Coordinator,* 19 (1970), 82-85.

Kirkendall, Lester A. *Premarital Intercourse and Interpersonal Relationships.* New York: Julian Press, 1961.

84

Reiss, Ira L. *Premarital Sexual Standards in America.* New York: Free Press, 1960.

Reiss, Ira L. *The Social Context of Premarital Sexual Permissiveness.* New York: Holt, Rinehart & Winston, 1967.

"Sexual passion is a matter of universal experience; and speaking broadly and generally, we may say it is a matter on which it is quite desirable that every adult at some time or other <u>should</u> have actual experience."

Edward Carpenter
(Quoted in Bloch, *The Sexual Life of Our Time,* 1937, p. 37)

CHAPTER 6

IMPOTENCE: WORRIES ABOUT "PERFORMANCE"

Impotence is a problem to many men from time to time, and some women are also concerned or involved, since this condition on the part of their husbands affects their sexual life too. Impotence usually refers to a man's being unable to attain or maintain an erection, thus interfering with his ability to perform sexual intercourse.

Sometimes impotency is divided into three different types: organic, functional, and psychogenic. The organic variety refers to impotency caused by some anatomical defect and is rather rare. Functional impotency may be the result of hormonal malfunction, or exhaustion, or excessive use of alcohol or drugs, and so on. Diabetes may affect some men's potency. Therefore if a man suffers from impotency over any extended period of time, he should have a physician check for diabetes as a precautionary measure.

The more frequent causes of impotency, however, are *psychogenic;* that is, the cause may lie not in any organic or physiological factor but rather in a man's head, in the kind of *thinking* he is doing about his sexual performance and other's expectations of him. Therefore, the man's head - or thinking - is what needs to be worked on, rather than his genitals.

Fear is perhaps one of the most frequent underlying causes of impotence. Fear of failure initiates a vicious circle, inhibiting a man's sexual performance after the first "failure," which may have been quite normal. That is, a man may not have been able to perform the sexual act in his usual manner and may not have been able to attain or maintain an erection basically because of physical exhaustion. However, because some men have a false idea that they should *always* be able to have an erection and maintain it for long periods of time, they therefore classify their temporary impotence as a "failure" and jump to the conclusion that they "are impotent," which they again falsely assume will last forever. Such thoughts or suspicions running through a man's mind on the next occasion he has for possible sexual intercourse will indeed practically insure that his penis will not respond in its usual fashion (but not because there is anything wrong with his penis, only his thinking).

Many men are too easily upset by their fear of not being able to perform the sex act adequately. They have the false idea that they should *always* be able to perform the sex act adequately (i.e., always be able to perform as a "stud"). If a woman indicates she is in any way displeased with a man's sexual performance, he may take this as "rejection" within himself, and this comes to mind as suggesting another possible failure on many a subsequent attempt at sexual intercourse.

We have seen in an earlier chapter how a man may be overly concerned about he size of his penis. He may assume (without consulting a professional member of the helping professions) that his penis is too small, and that, therefore, he will not be able to perform sexual intercourse sufficiently to satisfy the woman. That such fears are unfounded is rarely checked out, and so many men give up (assuming that they are irrevocably impotent) and never even try to make sexual overtures to a woman. His fear of being laughed at by the woman may indeed result in his being "impotent." But once he decides to investigate these matters and comes to understand the facts and get rid of some of his irrational expectations and assumptions, he can learn to function quite well sexually.

Fear of pregnancy may also cause impotence. Or, to be more precise, fear of causing pregnancy may cause impotence. Women are not the only ones who fear the possibility of pregnancy. I had a client whose fear of making his girl friend pregnant made him impotent.

He had a girl friend with whom he was in love and hoped to marry. She was willing to marry him, and both were interested in having premarital intercourse. She had invited him to her apartment on several occasions and indicated her willingness to have premarital intercourse with him. He was very attracted to her and when they danced he would frequently have an erection. But when the opportunity to have sexual intercourse presented itself, his penis went limp. He could not understand this and was very upset by his reactions. He felt that he and the girlfriend should not get married unless his impotence could be cured. The girlfriend agreed that they should not get married until after they had been able to have successful intercourse. He reported that the girlfriend was very understanding but he was afraid her patience might be wearing thin and that she might get disgusted with him and his impotence and call the marriage off.

I began to ask him what was going through his mind just prior to his impotent reaction. He related details of several occasions when, despite the opportunity for sex, and the desire on both his and her part, he simply could not maintain his erection long enough to even achieve the beginnings of intercourse.

When I asked him what thoughts went through his mind just prior to going to bed with his girl friend, he finally said that he was afraid that he would get her pregnant, and they were not in a position to marry at the present time. They hoped to be able to get married in a few years, but a pregnancy now would really foul things up.

When I asked him if she used any pills or any other birth control method, he admitted to me that he had never discussed the matter with her. That may seem amazing to anyone who thinks that such matters should be discussed, but I see many clients who get married without such discussions, who frequently have premarital intercourse without talking over what precautions need to be taken to prevent the possibility of pregnancy. Passion frequently overcomes reason in men-women relations.

This young man's concern for the young woman and his fear of getting her pregnant were the cause of his impotence. Or so it seemed to me on the basis of what he had revealed. So I suggested to him that had better discuss his fears with the young woman and specifically discuss birth control methods that they might use. He agreed that he would do so.

He later reported on his "homework assignment." he said he had asked his girl friend about birth control methods and she reported she used a diaphragm. After they had discussed the matter and were assured that the birth control method would prevent the pregnancy that neither wanted at this time, they were able to proceed to bed and have sexual intercourse, with no impotence on his part whatsoever.

Other causes of impotence are, for examples, feelings of inferiority or inadequacy and sometimes the fear of failure. It cannot be overemphasized that impotency occurs to almost all men occasionally, for a variety of reasons (not all of them deeply hidden in their psyches, either). We must not over psychologize and attribute deeply hidden, dark, sinister reasons for a man's occasional impotence.

As an example of their mistaken assumptions about sex and particularly impotence, many men believe falsely that, as they get older (say into their seventies) they have grown too old to function sexually. Some even convince themselves of this notion and, in effect, resign themselves to impotence and subsequently do not try to have intercourse anymore.

Older men who assume that they are impotent will nevertheless report to me that they have morning erections (which they believe to always be caused by a full bladder only) or they also occasionally report that they have an erection when aroused by dancing with a woman other than their wife. Such men obviously have the ability to have an erection. Their impotency may be situational; that is, they are impotent in a particular situation, with a particular sexual partner, but they may not be permanently impotent with all women for the rest of their lives, as they assume.

These false assumptions and misunderstandings about sex and impotence illustrate that impotence is to a large extent frequently psychological rather than physical in origin. [Some diseases, for example diabetes, can cause some problems with erections, of course. And some medications can have the side effect of adversely affecting erections.] Obviously, however, any man who has any question about his potency, should explore the physical possibilities before turning to a psychologist for help.

If a man has an understanding partner who is warm and loving, she can cooperate with the psychologist or marriage counselor or sex therapist and often be of the greatest help in aiding a man overcome his fear of impotence. If she can be relaxed and not push her partner, particularly being careful not to make unkind remarks or joke about his potency or virility (which, unfortunately, some wives do, I am sorry to say), she can be of great help to the therapist and give her partner the opportunity and the encouragement to try again with no pressure on his performance. Sex can be fun, even without orgasm every time for either partner, on occasion. Sex can be enjoyable, even when a man's erection is not as hard as it sometimes may be, or does not last quite as long as either partner might prefer. These thoughts are the sort that had better replace the irrational assumptions and self-defeating ideas that many men and women have about sex.

Another problem has come to be associated with impotency which may, in fact, not involve it at all. I refer to what is sometimes called "premature ejaculation." Sometimes some women have complained that their husbands have premature ejaculation when what is occurring is perfectly natural and normal. Once again it is a matter of wrong labeling or a misunderstanding of what is normal, natural sex.

The great majority of men report that they have ejaculation within two minutes of intromission, some within twenty seconds. When the evidence of length of time of sustained intromission in other animal species is considered, it puts much of what is termed "premature ejaculation" in better perspective. Tales of "endless intercourse" or "all night sessions" or intercourse for hours without end, had better be considered in the light that most sex occurs within a much shorter time span than these tall tales by "studs" who are willing to tell tales of sexual fantasy at the drop of a hat (or at least, as a minimum, the purchase of another beer at the local bar) would have us believe.

Sometimes so called "modern" books on sex may contribute to this misunderstanding surrounding so-called "premature ejaculation" by having readers believe that any man can go for hours if he just buys the book and employs the latest techniques described therein. Many such books need to be taken with a grain of salt. In fact, every book had better be read critically and checked out against the scientific evidence in the field. The dictum to read critically refers to *every* book, including this one. Because the Bible contains much misinformation and many unfortunate ideas about sex which continue to be believed merely because many people continue to read it uncritically, the Bible, too, had better be read thoughtfully, carefully and critically. It is not necessarily true merely because "It's in the book!"

In discussing impotence, some mention had perhaps be made of what has been termed *psuedo*impotence. This is sexual behavior which seems to be impotence but may not be. For example, a man who "loses" his erection too soon in an overly moist or over relaxed vagina (for example, one stretched by several childbirths) may assume that he is impotent when he actually is not. The vagina in such instances may not be providing the necessary stimulation. Sometimes vaginal surgery can help both partners enjoy sexual intercourse more.

There are other occasions which may provoke symptoms like those of impotence. One is vaginismus (strong muscular contractions within the vagina) which prevent intromission. Another is incomplete defloration (sometimes due to a particularly tough hymen) which may make coitus difficult. Still another example is where the wife is resistant or has an attitude which might be described as "unhelpful." Such conditions may lead the husband to a mild degree of impotence, but really do not indicate true impotence.

Young men who are having their first encounter with sexual intercourse sometimes experience impotence. If, for some reason or other, they are not successful during the first or even the second such opportunity, they may become exceedingly "gun-shy" and experience impotence on other occasions when the fear of failure runs through their minds again. This again is not irreversible impotence but rather something that can be overcome with the help of a professional person (a psychologist, marriage counselor or sex therapist, for example).

As was noted at the beginning of this chapter, some women may sometimes be involved in problems that some men may have with impotence, sometimes in effect as causative factors. Without subscribing totally to the psychoanalytic concept of the "castrating woman," one may note there are some women who incapacitate their husbands in many ways: by deriding them, perhaps without realizing it, by demeaning just about everything about them (their builds, their work, their virility, and so on). No woman can "castrate" a man in this psychological sense unless he allows her to do so, but it has been stated that impotence may be the defense of a husband who finds himself married to such a woman; impotence in such instances might be termed the last resort of the henpecked husband.

Another psychoanalytic concept concerns the "phallic woman," but once again we do not have to subscribe to all of the psychoanalytic assumptions to admit that there are some women who manipulate and arrange all things in life, including the sexual life of their husbands: they arrange positions, specify the time, place, and conditions under which sex will occur (and not occur), prescribing and proscribing movements and techniques, and even regulating the number and strengths of the sexual thrusts the husband may make in sexual intercourse. Such women may think they are merely "training" their husbands to become "good" and "proper" lovers; they may succeed, only too often, in merely depriving themselves (through having husbands who, understandably under these sorts of conditions, develop "impotence"). And sometimes these very wives wonder why!

Of course, it goes without saying that unthinking husbands can also turn off their wives to sex by their own "wham-bam" tactics; we shall take up such matters in the chapter on preorgasmic women. The older term, "frigidity", can on occasion be the wife's response to unthinking behavior on the part of the husband.

Some men have impotency problems which seem to be related to overwork. Such cases occur frequently in men who are sometimes middle-aged and in creative and responsible positions. The overwork may sound like an excuse, but work frequently can be sometimes the most important factor in their lives at this point and one that they give up very reluctantly, if at all. Many men in our culture have bought the Puritan work ethic, whether they know it as such or not, and hard work is their credo, even when it has an adverse effect on their sex lives.

Sometimes such men, who claim overwork as the cause of their impotency, have really developed a lessened desire for their wives, and use this more "acceptable" reason of overtiredness from overwork as their excuse. Of course, some men really are deeper into their work at this time in their lives and have wives who may have, sometimes, practically abandoned their husbands for their children. Under such conditions, impotency may really occur as anhedonia (or lack of sexual desire) rather than true impotence. The appearance of another attractive woman on the scene, be it the proverbial secretary or co-worker or some other available female, may prove the impotence to be quite temporary. For other men, of course, overwork and the impending possibility of bankruptcy may continue to be a valid concern and the cause of impotency.

The fact that a man may be impotent with his wife but not with another woman points up what might be called "selective" impotence. That is, what has occurred is not the true variety but anhedonia which is perceived erroneously as impotence. What is called impotence, then, may be an unverbalized rejection of, or fear of, or waning attraction to, a particular sexual partner.

Some men develop what others would consider "fantastic" ideas about sex and particularly about the vagina, and these irrational ideas may cause impotence as a somewhat protective measure. For example, some men develop what has been termed "castration anxiety" in which they imagine the vagina has something like teeth in it, or is like a snapping turtle, and can thus damage their penis.

Less esoteric but much more common as causes of impotence are deep-seated hostility toward or fear of women in general. Some men just do not like women. This obviously interferes with an adequate sex life.

Men who have such negative reactions to women sometimes turn to homosexuality for sexual release. In striving to "justify" their homosexuality, such men may try to have intercourse with a woman, find that they are impotent in that situation, and thus conclude (erroneously) that, since they are impotent with women, they must be homosexual. We shall discuss homosexuality in more detail in a later chapter. Here we only want to show that impotence with a woman has been used by some men as an excuse for turning to the so-called "gay" life.

Wives of impotent men can be of great help in the therapeutic treatment of impotency. In fact, some authorities advise that treatment of impotent men should only be attempted when the wives are also willing to cooperate and participate along with their husbands. Whether or not one goes along with this dictum, the importance of the wife in such cases cannot be overlooked. Wives can clearly sabotage any therapeutic efforts by talking about their husbands' sexual difficulties. Conjoint sessions with both partners can touch on just such matters and help the wife understand her contributions, both negative and positive.

Husbands had better understand, as do wives, that an erection *cannot be willed into existence.* It is a natural reaction and essentially involuntary. Many things can interfere with an erection taking place. Such interferences can occur in the middle years of even the healthiest, emotionally well-balanced men. And interferences can occur in very young men who are having their initial sexual encounters. If both men and women can learn that sometimes men do have difficulties in achieving and maintaining an erection, despite the desire to have sex on the part of both partners, then both partners can adopt a more relaxed attitude toward sex play and enjoy sex, even when impotence sometimes occurs. It is no catastrophe unless it is arbitrarily defined as such by either partner.

If we adopt the attitude that we can learn from our mistakes as well as our successes (sometimes more from the former than from the latter), then we can do away with the usual arbitrary definitions of "failure" which are thought of as impotence. Sexual experiences do not have to be always romantically "perfect," they can be enjoyable and fun when considerably less than "perfect." Giving up romantic notions can help sex be more fun.

In the treatment of impotency reported by Masters and Johnson (1970, p. 213), the two factors which were associated with the highest levels of treatment failure were religious orthodoxy and homosexual orientation. If impotency is to be adequately treated, these two factors are the greatest opposition and therefore had better be overcome. Many people in both camps will not appreciate this conclusion but the facts speak for themselves.

Impotency is a problem largely (but not entirely, of course) for psychological reasons and therefore can be treated psychologically, provided the clients are willing to attack and get rid of their self-defeating, irrational assumptions and ideas. It is a difficult but not impossible task.

SUGGESTED FURTHER READING

Ard, Ben N., Jr. "Seven Ways to Enjoy Sex More," *Sexology*, 35 (1969), 508-510.

Crider, Blake. "Situational Impotence," *in* M. F. Demartino (Editor) *Sexual Behavior and Personality Characteristics* (New York: Citadel Press, 1963), pp. 290-301).

Harper, Robert A. "Overcoming Impotence," *Sexology*, 31 (1965), 680-682.

Kelly, G. Lombard. "Impotence," *in* Albert Ellis & Albert Abarbanel (Editors) *The Encyclopedia of Sexual Behavior* (New York: Hawthorn Books, 1961), pp. 515-527.

Masters, William H. & Johnson, Virginia E. *Human Sexual Inadequacy* (Boston: Little, Brown, 1970), pp. 137-213.

McCary, James L. *Human Sexuality* (Princeton, N.J.: Van Nostrand, 1967), pp. 296-302.

Oliven, John F. *Sexual Hygiene and Pathology* (Philadelphia: Lippincott, 2nd edition, 1965), pp. 422-452.

"Sexual adjustment inheres in psychic adaptation far more than in genital or reproductive structure."

Robert L. Dickinson, M.D.
(Quoted in Wile, *The Sex Life of the Unmarried Adult*, 1934, p. 209)

CHAPTER 7

"FRIGIDITY" OR CHANGING FROM "COLD" TO "WARM"

Frigidity is a problem to many women in our culture and necessarily, therefore, to the men in their lives. Unfortunately the label "frigid" probably causes more trouble and misunderstandings than just about any other term in sexology. I have come to the point in my practice that I practically never introduce the term because of its unfortunate effect and the misunderstandings that arise therefrom. But the term is still commonly used by many people, both male and female, and therefore we shall discuss it here.

Too many women have been labeled "frigid," meaning totally incapable of an adequate sexual response, when in fact they are neither. I have had women in my office labeled as "frigid" when what was meant was not that the woman in question was totally incapable of responding sexually but merely that she was unresponsive or "cold." I have had women clients label themselves as "frigid" merely because they have not responded to their husbands in ways they assume they should (that is, as their husbands say they should, or as they assume other women do in similar circumstances).

One woman client of mine reported her problem as follows: "I guess I'm frigid." When I asked her why she thought she was frigid she said, "My husband thinks so." When I asked if she had ever had sexual intercourse with a man other than her husband, she replied no. My next question was "Then how do you know whether you are truly frigid or not?" Of course she did not know whether she was or not, since she had no basis for

104

comparison or even any real knowledge of what frigidity really is all about. What are the relevant facts about frigidity?

The causes of frigidity may be grouped into three major categories: organic causes, relationship causes, and psychological causes. I have come to assume that men and women have basically very similar sexual desires and drives, although there are obviously many individual differences, particularly where cultural influences may impinge on how people integrate sex in their lives. But as a matter of fact, some women seem to be able to live without sex in a somewhat easier fashion than most men. If we want to label women who seem to have little or no sexual desire as "frigid," we may of course do so. But outside of the rather rare organic cases where the sex organs have been defective from birth, most women, I believe, develop normal sexual desires as they grow into maturity. The factors which can inhibit their showing any sexual desire are largely cultural, in my opinion.

One of the organic factors that can cause sexual reactions which might be called anesthetic or hormonal deficiencies. Certain diseases can interfere with the more normal expression of sexual desires. Examples are diabetes, anemia, or leukemia. Any woman who has any question about her own sexual normality should, of course, rule out any organic factors by checking with her physician. However, virtually all authorities agree that most cases of frigidity result from *psychological* rather than organic or physical factors. Still, a checkup with a physician can prevent the error of over psychologizing. And after the physical checkup has ruled out any organic factors, then one can begin to look for other possibilities: that is, relationship or psychological causes.

Humans interact sexually usually within the context of a

relationship, and the quality of this relationship can affect the sexual responses. This seems particularly the case with women more than men, in our culture. That is, responses that some people would call "frigid" may be evidenced when the women in a relationship becomes worried about her husband's attitudes or responses. If some women feel that love is no longer in the relationship, they may become "frigid," or at least evidence "colder" sexual responses than formerly.

One client of mine "turned off" as far as sex was concerned when her husband came home drunk. Other wives have become "frigid" when they discovered that their husbands have been unfaithful. Still other wives become "frigid" when they resent what their husbands do to them in their sexual relations. In these cases, and in other similar ones, the wife may be said to be "frigid" in a relative sense, that is, she is frigid with regard to her husband, or in this particular relationship. She may not be totally frigid, necessarily. In another relationship, with another man with whom she has greater rapport, she may recover and overcome her previous frigidity. Sometimes, when marriage counseling helps overcome some of the marital problems, frigid responses can be rectified even in the ongoing relationship, if both partners are willing and able to work through problems.

Among some women there may be psychological causes for their apparent frigidity, which may stem from feelings of guilt or shame about sex, usually learned as they were growing up in this culture, with its many distorted and sick ideas about sex. Sometimes these early learnings, frequently half-forgotten, continue to plague women long after they are grown and married and have had several children. I have known clients who would curtail the frequency of their sexual intercourse when they were visiting the parental home over the holidays because they did not want their parents to hear them having sexual relations. This attitude of subservience to parental attitudes can even apply to smoking and drinking as well as sex. I have had clients who, while visiting their family of origin, would only sneak a cigarette in the bathroom. Others would stash a bottle of liquor perhaps in the garage and then sneak out there to have a quick drink unbeknownst to their parents. All this sort of behavior illustrates that too many adults have not resolved their relationships with their parents and still allow the latter to dictate what sort of behavior is acceptable or not. (Ard, 1983)

Some women seem to fear the (to them) apparent loss of self-control which seems to them to be involved in really letting go in their sexual relations. I have had several such clients who sometimes think that any such letting go means giving up too much power to the male. Some women have picked up ideas that females should be very careful never to let themselves go, because that would mean giving the men in their lives the right to say when they (the women) can have sexual satisfaction. Some writers in the women's liberation movement may have contributed to this unfortunate idea which causes some women to become frigid and thus defeat their own ends. Obviously not all members of the women's liberation movement are haters of men, though some seem to be. The following excerpt from the SCUM (Society for Cutting Up Men) Manifesto will illustrate this extremely negative attitude toward males:

> *"Life in this society being, at best, an utter*
> *bore and no aspect of society being at all relevant to*
> *women, there remains to civic-minded, responsible, thrill-*

*seeking females only to overthrow the government,
eliminate the money system, institute complete automation,
and destroy the male sex.* " (Solanis, 1970, p. 514)

But some cooperation with a man would seem to be a very basic ingredient in any sexual satisfactory relationship for women. Otherwise, a simple battery-operated vibrator would serve just as well, if not better, than a man. But a satisfying sexual relationship means some, hopefully enjoyable, cooperation between the man and woman involved. Both had better learn to give to each other, at least some of the time, in order to have mutually pleasurable and satisfying sexual relations.

Thus varying degrees of frigidity result from the anti-sex attitudes which are still prevalent in our culture, despite all the talk of the sexual revolution supposedly going on all around us at the present time. Too many women who might be said to fall into the "frigid" category are still indoctrinated with unfortunate attitudes toward sex. The typical conventional attitudes toward sex are still irrational and very self-defeating. (Ard, *Rational Sex Ethics,* 1989) The sex therapist's job is to get his clients to de-indoctrinate themselves, that is, to get rid of these self-defeating attitudes, these irrational ideas about sex.

To illustrate how a woman can develop habits and attitudes which may contribute to frigidity, consider the following client's story. This young, college-educated woman had gone with her future husband for some time before they had married. They had gone steady and petted extensively before marriage. Yet they had mutually agreed not to have premarital intercourse. So they developed a pattern of petting which always stopped just short of sexual intercourse, that is, putting the penis into the vagina.

108

When they finally got married, she reported that there seemed to be a "wall" erected which, in effect, prevented her from enjoying sexual intercourse. She said she enjoyed all the foreplay, all the lovemaking; she (like many other women in our culture) seemed to like the foreplay better than the actual sex act. She apparently could not have an orgasm now that sex was permissible in their eyes because she had developed the habit of being satisfied with the preliminaries. She did not actually enjoy coitus. She desired "sex," that is, all the foreplay, but did not enjoy sexual intercourse, that is, penis in the vagina.

Such a woman might be termed frigid; however, there was nothing wrong with her organically. [As is my pattern in such cases, I had her checked out with a physician colleague before starting to work with her myself.] Her main problem was that she had arbitrarily defined only certain aspects of the sexual act as acceptable (due to the pressure from our culture against premarital sex relations), and even when she became married, and sexual intercourse was now presumably all right, she had to unlearn her sexual responses and learn to look forward to sexual intercourse, to actually want and seek to have the penis in the vagina. The "wall" she had erected in her mind is an example of the price we pay in this society for regarding premarital intercourse as the terrible sin or catastrophe that many conventionally religious people do. Parents indoctrinate their daughters to avoid premarital intercourse at all costs, and then we wonder why we have so many cases of frigidity!

A distinction may be made between feelings of shame or inadequacy and feelings of guilt (or sinfulness or worthlessness). (Ard, 1983) Some parents seem to stress approaches which emphasize shame and thus encourage fears of inadequacy in their daughters when it comes to sexual performance. Other parents stress the sinful aspect and instill guilt reactions in their daughters which frequently last for many years. Both such forms of indoctrination contribute to frigidity in too many women in our culture.

Some men can contribute to the frigidity of their wives by the way they approach sex. Some stories about rather horrible experiences on the wedding night are not too uncommon in my practice. Some men have been led to believe that they should assert their masculinity or virility through a strong, aggressive "rape" type scene on their wedding night. Such men may have tremendous ignorance about sexual matters, despite the fact that they are supposed to be the one member of the pair who has the all-important sexual knowledge (according to some presumptions in our culture). Some such men believe that they should break the hymen with one stroke. Such thoughtlessness has indeed turned off many a woman on her wedding night. No better evidence is needed for more scientific sex education in our public schools than just this sort of ignorant behavior.

Some men may contribute to the frigidity of their wives by insisting that there is one and only one right way to have sex. They approach sex consistently in this rigid fashion, and they are frequently surprised when I point out in therapy sessions that such an approach may be contributing to that very frigidity in their wives of which they complain bitterly about. But fortunately men can learn new ideas and new approaches to sex and help their wives become more relaxed and therefore able to overcome their frigidity. It obviously takes much hard work on the part of the women to overcome their previous negative indoctrination, too. Any woman with frigidity as a problem can learn to focus on her own sexual desires and wishes, to relax and enjoy sex, and to eradicate from her previous thinking all the self-defeating ideas, assumptions, and unquestioned teachings which she has absorbed from our culture. Perhaps the hardest part of her task is learning to go against what she frequently learned from her mother.

Frigidity as syndrome may actually be a mixture of several different sorts of problems. There may be a problem of sexual anhedonia, or lack of interest in sex, for example, specifically the absence of desire for sexual intercourse. Or there may be sexual anesthesia, which is the inability to experience pleasurable feelings during sexual intercourse. Finally, there may be what might be termed true frigidity, which is the inability to reach orgasm during intercourse.

The lack of interest in sex reveals itself in various ways. Some women show little desire before they are married, and seem to get along all right sexually with their husbands during the period when they are married (perhaps several years), but then when they lose their husbands (through divorce or death), they seem able to go for relatively long periods, perhaps even years, without any problem from the lack of sex. They actually seem to lose all desire for sex, or at least act as if they have no sexual desire. How much of this is true sexual anhedonia or a form of frigidity is hard to say. Some of this sort of behavior may be a cultural thing. For example, these women may have sexual desires but, because of the influence of the culture, they give little or no evidence of any sexual desire. Some of the syndrome may, of course, be true frigidity or simply sexual anhedonia; that is, these women simply do not have strong sexual desires. They can take it or leave it, either way, without much bother.

Sometimes women in this category may never make sexual overtures to their husbands, and therefore there may be long periods of no sexual activity. They have on occasion said in my office, "But I never deny him sex." Such a woman has the attitude that her husband can have sex anytime he wants it; he just has to ask for it, as one client told me. These are the women who look upon sex in marriage as their conjugal duty or obligation. They assume they should never deny their husband sex, and they act accordingly. But this does not mean that they give much indication of having any strong sexual desires themselves.

Other women with little sexual desire may "freeze up" when their husbands approach them sexually, or adopt the attitude of "get it over and done with as soon as possible." Such women may have sex very infrequently and may be even accepting of the fact that their husband satisfies his sexual desires elsewhere. I had one client of this type who even told her husband in one of our joint sessions to "get his sex elsewhere." Unfortunately her husband took the position that his wife's love for him could only be measured by the frequency with which she gave him sex. Obviously these two had a serious problem about the meaning of sex in their lives.

Sometimes the lack of sexual desire seems to result from an operation such as hysterectomy. Women who evidence this response, and thus "give up" on sex afterwards, have equated sex with reproduction entirely, and feel that sex with no chance of reproduction is unseemly or improper. There is wide agreement among the authorities in such matters that any diminishing of sexual desire after such an operation (where the uterus but not the ovaries are removed) is the result of psychogenic factors and is not inherent in the operation itself. Such women had better redefine the meaning of sex in their lives. There is no reason that sex need be over after such an operation.

Similar freezing out of the sexual aspect of life after an operation has been seen in some women who have had breasts removed because of cancer. Once again the operation in and of itself need not remove sex from the women's life. I have had cases where the woman was so ashamed of her looks after the operation that she ruled out any opportunity for sexual intercourse because of what she *assumed* would be the male's reactions to her lack of breasts. Now there is no doubt that many men in this culture have made beauty of breasts an important aspect of the sexual attractiveness of the women in their lives. But *not all* men have this same attitude; there are men who can and do have frequent sexual intercourse with women who have had their breasts removed. That such things are possible does not enter the realm of the woman's thinking who has had a double mastectomy, and so she rules sex out of her life henceforth.

Perhaps one of the most general factors in frigidity of the sexual anesthesia type (referring to the absence of pleasure during sexual intercourse) may be attributed to a frequently deep-seated aversion to, or fear of, men and sex generally. Obviously where a woman fears that she will experience pain rather than pleasure, she naturally is not very interested in having much sex. Where the husband cooperates in such cases,however, and is a thoughtful, gentle, tender man, many cases of frigidity of this sort can be overcome. The wife, of course, has her homework assignments cut out for her in such cases: she had better learn to root out of her mind any irrational assumptions about men and sex which are preventing her from realizing a normal sex life.

Sometimes this sort of problem is more difficult in single women who have never had any sexual experience and, because of their *assumed* frigidity, abandon any hopes of a normal sex life before they have attempted to resolve or check out any of their ideas about sex and men. Encouraging such women to try out new experiences with men, including sexual ones, is not an easy task because of their fears. But I have had single women who had decided they were going to be "old maids" try, and try again, and after some not so good experiences, keep working on their self-defeating attitudes, overcome them, and manage to integrate sex in their lives in a meaningful way. Overcoming the influences of the past and one's earlier moral teachings can be accomplished with satisfying results if one is willing to do the hard work involved. Changing one's whole philosophy of life is what is sometimes involved and that is not an easy task. But with hard work and risking one's self, one can develop a new philosophy of life which may prove more satisfying and less self-defeating. (Ard, 1983)

Overcoming the inhibitions that our culture traditionally imposes on so many women is a necessary task if one truly wants to resolve the problems of frigidity. Some people assume that women are "just naturally" modest, chaste, inhibited, reserved, passive, and all the other middle-class "virtues" that are conventionally associated with the female sex. But these sorts of behavior are not inherited but, on the contrary, are culturally *learned. Therefore they can be unlearned.* Psychotherapy can help.

While we are discussing frigidity we should mention that there is a phenomenon known as pseudofrigidity. In this condition the woman may deprive herself of orgasm or the primary factor may be the frequently perfunctory way in which the husband performs the sexual act with his wife. In some such cases the woman, because of early training, may be so shy and inhibited that she has difficulty allowing her husband to perform the foreplay required to adequately prepare her for exciting or even satisfactory sexual intercourse. Other women who may fall in this category may have been left "high and dry" so often, with their sexual desires left unfulfilled, that they usually anticipate this happening again and consequently remain frigid.

One of the most common failings with regard to frigidity is the lack of adequate communication between husband and wife. I have had clients who have had regular and frequent intercourse for twenty or thirty years of marriage but who had never discussed sex. So many couples just *have* sex and *assume* that everything is all right. I have to get my clients to *stop assuming and start asking*. People who are going to make adequate love to each other had better check out what their partners actually desire in the lovemaking, rather than just assuming they already know.

I have had wives say to me that they assume their husbands know when they (the wives) want sex and yet, when I ask, "Do you tell your husband when you desire sex?' they are frequently shocked and say, "Of course not!" Then I ask, "Well, how is he supposed to know that you desire sex?" And I have actually had wives say, "By looking into my eyes." I have had to tell many clients that husbands cannot read their wives' minds, that the proverbial "gleam" in anyone's eye, male or female, may very easily be misread, or missed entirely. Sexual partners had better talk explicitly to each other and tell each other what the nonverbal signs are, and better yet, tell each other how they want their loving done. That is, they should not be afraid to use their lips for more than mere kisses and tell their partners very explicitly just how they want their loving done, as well as when and where.

Some men have been led to believe that they alone are entirely to blame if their wives are frigid. Even though they may have read some books about sex, and have had some sexual experiences (and even think of themselves as good lovers), if their wives are frigid, they may assume that they (the husbands) have just not mastered the right specific techniques. On some occasions, such may be the case. But more often than not the origin of much frigidity lies in the wives' heads (not their genitals), that is, in their false assumptions and irrational ideas about sex.

Only when these erroneous ideas have been challenged and changed and eradicated may the best of techniques of any husband be put to good use. Sometimes the so-called "modern" marriage manuals have led to the false idea that it is always the husband's lack of proper technique that causes the wife's frigidity.

We have already seen how, in fact, a husband can contribute to a wife's frigidity, but that is not usually the whole story. Some women are their own worst enemy as far as achieving sexual satisfaction is concerned. They can learn to achieve such satisfaction (even though their husband is not the world's greatest lover) if they can learn to focus better, relax more, be more explicit with their partner, and root out every last vestige of irrational thoughts, assumptions, and unquestioned premises about sex.

SUGGESTED FURTHER READING

Ard, Ben N., Jr. "How to Stimulate Erotic Zones," *Sexology,* 37 (1971) 4-6.

Ard, Ben N., Jr. "Communication in Marriage," *Rational Living,* 5
    (1971), 20-22.

Ard, Ben N., Jr. *Living Without Guilt and/or Blame: Conscience, Superego
    and Psychotherapy* (Smithtown, N.Y.: Exposition Press, 1983).

Ard, Ben N., Jr. *Rational Sex Ethics* (New York: Peter Lang
    Publishing, 1989).

Ellis, Albert. "How Males Contribute to Females' Frigidity," *in* Albert Ellis,
    Sex Without Guilt (New York: Lyle Stuart, 1958), pp. 115-127.

Hastings, D. W. *Impotence and Frigidity* (Boston: Little, Brown, 1963).

Oliven, John F. "Frigidity," *in* John F. Oliven. *Sexual Hygiene and
Pathology*   (Philadelphia: Lippincott, 1965), pp. 453-476.

Solanis, Valerie. Excerpts from the SCUM (Society for the Cutting Up of
    Men) Manifesto, *in* Robin Morgan (Editor) *Sisterhood Is Powerful*
    (New York: Vintage Books, 1970), pp. 514-519.

*". . .to the free course of her sensations, to the fulfillment of all
her longings, to the natural issue of the most natural of all impulses,
innumerable obstacles are imposed, which make the woman a slave to the
thoughts of others and to numerous short-sighted and irrational
conventions."*

Bernhard A. Bauer

Woman and Love (1927, vol. 1, p. 44)

CHAPTER 8

ORGASM PROBLEMS: PREORGASMIC WOMEN

In the sorts of problems that women clients bring to the helping professions, one set is of fairly recent origin and may have been somewhat brought on, to some extent, by some sexologists and writers in the field themselves. These are the problems of orgasm, complaints about which are very common of late. Clients are generally concerned about not having simultaneous orgasms every time the partners have sexual intercourse. Both men and women may be concerned about whether or not the woman has a "clitoral" versus a "vaginal" orgasm. These questions are intertwined with ones about impotence and frigidity, of course. But because of the rising interest in such matters, orgasm problems perhaps deserve special treatment in a separate chapter.

In days gone by it was traditionally thought that women were not even supposed to have much sexual enjoyment, let alone orgasm, during sexual intercourse. This applied to "nice" women, in this earlier view, of course. In these psychologically sophisticated days, however, since the so-called sexual revolution and the women's liberation movement, not to mention the smattering of Freud that many people think they have, women are demanding equality with men in just about everything, including the sexual sphere, and particularly as to orgasm.

So female orgasm is now discussed in marriage manuals in great detail, so that literate women who read such manuals are now aware of the fact that they *should* be having orgasms. In fact, the height of sexual delight or the peak experience in the sexual realm is thought to be "simultaneous orgasm," wherein the male ejaculates and the female has her orgasm at exactly the same moment. This supposedly defines the proper conclusion to an adequately conducted sex act.

The marriage manuals have perhaps oversold the concept of the simultaneous orgasm. With increasing numbers of books being written about sex, we have reached, perhaps, the ultimate absurdity wherein male and female retire to bed with the sex manual in one hand and stop-watch in the other, hoping to reach that elusive "nirvana," simultaneous orgasm. Not only is simultaneous orgasm viewed as a sometime thing which may bring great delight and enjoyment, it is too often these days, it would seem, made into a prerequisite, or used to define any satisfactory sexual act. Such an act is thus assumed to be a failure if simultaneous orgasm is not achieved. This amounts to an arbitrary definition of the adequate sex act, much too perfectionistic, and is therefore ultimately self-defeating and detrimental to satisfactory and enjoyable sexual relations.

As a psychologist, sexologist, and marriage counselor, I have been seeing too many couples of late who are hung up on this false, perfectionistic ideal of simultaneous orgasm. I believe others in the helping professions would concur. What seems to be needed is a little more perspective and clearer understanding of female orgasm and the changing expectations regarding sex between men and women in the sophisticated culture of today.

In view of the fact that many women have difficulty reaching orgasm *every* time they have sexual intercourse, it would seem on the fact of it self-defeating for both females and males to expect or demand that simultaneous orgasm *always* be the end result of sexual intercourse. As a matter of fact, it may be self-defeating for a woman or a man even to expect that the woman will have *an orgasm* ever time sexual intercourse takes place. Such expectations are just unrealistic.

Sexual intercourse can be a delightful, enjoyable experience in a variety of ways, even without the woman necessarily *always* having an orgasm. This would seem to be a psychologically healthier expectation than the arbitrary demand or expectation that the woman always have an orgasm. It is certainly more realistic.

Seeking simultaneous orgasm may be a legitimate aim well worth working toward in sexual relations. But demanding it, or expecting it as practically a definition of a "complete" sex act, is asking too much, it would seem. Many women assume that they are frigid if they cannot achieve simultaneous orgasm every time while having sexual intercourse with their sexual partner. Many men assume that they are "failures" as lovers if they cannot bring their sexual partner to a simultaneous orgasm every time they have sexual intercourse. Both of these foregoing assumptions had better be questioned, challenged, and eliminated, if the sexual intercourse is to have a better chance of being an enjoyable, satisfying experience. *Demanding* things in the sexual area, like many other areas in life, frequently proves very self-defeating.

If sex is, on the other hand, accepted as capable of bringing a wide variety of pleasant sensations, feelings, and reactions, then the couple can relax and not feel bad or assume that they are, in some sense, sexual "failures" or "duds" simply because they do not always achieve that elusive simultaneous orgasm. Assuming this more flexible attitude toward sex will prove more productive of sound, satisfying sexual relations than the perfectionistic striving for simultaneous-orgasm-at-all-costs sort of attitude.

As a matter of fact, with a more realistic and relaxed attitude on the part of both male and female, the male helps the female to have (on occasion) multiple orgasms (none of which may be exactly simultaneous with his). This having multiple orgasms can be very satisfying to a woman, and may, on occasion, be even more appreciated by her than a simultaneous orgasm.

Sex acts can be rollicking good times, rambunctious, and even hilarious on occasion. One client of mine fell out of bed and broke an arm as a result of such a frolicsome good time. But sex acts can also be rather quiet, relaxing and contented times, with just a good deal of warmth and holding of each other in comforting, loving arms. Some orgasms have been described as real "peak experiences" which may have a revivifying effect. (Maslow, 1970, pp. 164-165) Other orgasms seem to ring relatively few bells; the earth does not always shake. Yet such orgasms are still valued.

Too often when simultaneous orgasm is not achieved by those striving perfectionistically to be "sexual athletes," the question frequently reduces down to whether one of the other of the partners is to blame - that is, "Whose *fault* is it?" *Blaming* either partner for failing to achieve simultaneous orgasm is a needlessly self-defeating pattern that can have a devastating effect on sexual relations. Some wives have complained by saying , "How does it happen that men (who are supposed, traditionally, to know all about sex) are unable to bring their wives to a climax?" This question asked in this way, seeming to blame men for the women's lack of the attainment of orgasm misses the basic point that the attainment of orgasm by women requires the active, thoughtful participation of *both* partners. [The same thing may be said for the man reaching an orgasm.] The woman not achieving an orgasm cannot justifiably always be blamed on the man alone. In fact, *blaming* is rarely ever helpful, no matter who is blamed.

Techniques can be learned which may prove helpful. But the whole point of mechanistically applying various "techniques" may obscure a more basic idea, and that is that the success of the various techniques depends upon many factors, including the quality of the relationship between the partners and their effective communication (both verbal and non-verbal). The most ingenious techniques may fail completely if one partner resents or rejects the other, or if either (or both) perfectionistically demand stopwatch accuracy in arriving at simultaneous orgasm.

The question of whether women have two distinct and different kinds of orgasm, "clitoral" and "vaginal," is one that has come to bother some sophisticated, literate women (and some men) in recent years. This may be another sexual problem which has been contributed to, if not somewhat caused by, some of the authorities in the field.

Since Freud started this whole concern, perhaps we should say the he believed (and taught a lot of other people to believe) that women first start out having an orgasm through masturbation, which usually involves stimulation of the clitoris. (Hence this was termed "clitoral" orgasm.) Freud believed, however, that in order to assure adequate sexual functioning in marriage a woman had to learn to achieve orgasm through sexual intercourse (and specifically this meant through intromission of the penis into the vagina). Women who remained "fixated" on the clitoris as the only means of achieving orgasm they were willing to consider were assumed by Freudians to have not "fully developed." A "mature" woman, in this Freudians view, is one who can transfer from having "clitoral" orgasms to having "vaginal" orgasms.

As marriage manuals, books on sex techniques, and other literature put forth this Freudian idea, many women have evidently come to assume that they were "frigid" or "immature," or in some way sexual inadequate, since they could often not achieve orgasm merely thorough sexual intercourse alone. In other words, they might well be able to achieve a clitoral orgasm but they were apparently unable to achieve a vaginal orgasm.

Recent research (Masters and Johnson, 1961) has come to the conclusion that orgasm is orgasm, no matter how achieved. The conclusion may help relieve those women's minds who have worried unnecessarily about this matter.

More specifically, some authorities (Ellis, 1963) have suggested that the vaginal orgasm is a myth. If, as Masters and Johnson (1961) have shown in their research, women achieve orgasm in a variety of ways (through stimulation of *various* parts of their bodies, not just the clitoris or the vagina), and the resulting orgasm they achieve is essentially the same (that is, the total physiological response is the same, no matter how triggered), then perhaps women would be better off if they ceased their unnecessary worrying abut "how" they achieve orgasm.

Some women may be stimulated to the point of orgasm by the caressing of their breasts, others can apparently have their breasts caressed endlessly and never achieve an orgasm that way. Some of my women clients have told me that they prefer to have orgasm through penis in the vagina rather than stimulating their clitoris with a mechanical vibrator. Some women like to have their ears nibbled; others find this sort of thing does practically nothing for them except, perhaps, irritate them. All in all, these various individual differences show that many women achieve orgasms through having various portions of their bodies stimulated. And if they are willing to experiment, relax, and learn new approaches, they can have more than one way to achieve orgasms.

Husbands, also, need not blame themselves unnecessarily because their wives do not achieve orgasm through mere intercourse. If the husband can bring his wife to the point of having an orgasm through manipulation of her clitoris, fine. He may help her to have multiple orgasms in this fashion.

For some women, changing positions to only a small degree (for example, putting her knees over her husband's shoulders in the usual position of man above the woman) may enable sufficient penetration and stimulation to occur to afford the woman orgasm. The deeper penetration may push and pull the clitoris and thus aid orgasm even though the clitoris is not touched directly.

In spite of the fact that many women in our culture seem to have more orgasm problems then men do, I still believe, in a very fundamental sense, that women have just as great a potentiality for orgasm as men. In fact, they apparently have a greater potentiality for multiple orgasms than most men. Therefore, the major difficulty in orgasm problems of many women in our culture probably lies primarily in the psychological realm rather than in the physiological realm.

Our culture lays a greater degree of sexual repression and inhibition upon women than men, and these psychocultural influences would seem to be the primary factors which interfere with some women's ability to achieve orgasm. This does not deny the individual differences to be found among women (as well as among men) with regard to sexual drive, desire, and quickness of response.

I have seen too many female clients who have orgasm problems, not because they are physiologically incapable of having orgasms, but rather because of such psychological factors as fears of being injured by the penis, fear of letting themselves go completely in intercourse, fear of pregnancy and childbirth. Other women clients of mine have been married to men who lacked adequate skill or tenderness or patience, and these factors have also contributed to orgasm problems for women.

The hopeful thing abut these above-mentioned factors is that, since they are psychological in nature, many if not most of them can be changed with psychological help. The basic problems in most cases is in the psyche, not the genitals.

Therefore, if the woman who has orgasm problems can free herself from the blanket of psychological inhibition our culture has laid on her, she probably will be capable of responding through a more effective use of her mind to the degree necessary to achieve orgasm more of the time. Focusing on sexually stimulating thoughts and images in her mind can aid her achieve more frequent orgasm. (Some women have been able to achieve orgasm without even touching themselves anywhere on their body but merely by thinking sexy thoughts, erotic thoughts, and dwelling on what brings them sexual pleasure.)

Some women have been liberated somewhat from previous inhibitions by seeing some of the recent films and videos that depict sex in a frank, open way. Some people with fundamental religious backgrounds call any such films "pornographic"; but be that as it may, use of such films open up possibilities and develop a more experimental attitude and approach toward sexuality has proved helpful with some of my clients. I have recommended certain films - not all the type called "hard-core" pornographic, either- which some of my women clients have reported has turned them on to sexuality in a more open, healthy fashion than had their previous upbringing. One client reported that the film "Ryan's Daughter" presented sex in a new light to her and that she went home after the film eager to adopt a more open, healthy attitude toward sex with her husband.

I have recommended some poetry to some female clients who had rather inhibited views of sex. One book of free verse, "This Is My Beloved," by Walter Benton, is one I have recommended to several of my women clients. Some of them return after reading the book and say, "Dr. Ard, why did you recommend that dirty book to me?" Others have said, softly, "I wish I had a man who would write that sort of poetry for me." Obviously, the latter response argues well for a woman being more open to sexual expression, while the former response shows that a lot of work still needs to be done.

Some women who are ashamed of their bodies have difficulty going nude and letting themselves go completely in the sex act. One client asked if it was all right for her to keep her nightgown on during intercourse with her husband. When asked why she wanted to do this, she said it was because she was ashamed of the way her body looked now. She had some stretch marks from having several babies and she did not want her husband to see the marks (which she thought of as "scars") on her stomach. After she had worked through her feelings, thoughts and assumptions about this matter, she later presented her husband with a replica of the "The Kiss" by Rodin (like the one I have in my office) with a little note saying that she wished that they could make love looking like the couple in the sculpture. But everyone grows older over time, and nearly everyone gets grayer, with more lines; the breasts eventually sag, many men develop "pots," and so on. And part of a healthy response to these facts of life is not to let one's assumptions about them interfere with a good, healthy sexual adjustment.

Men seem, in general, to have relatively less problems with orgasm than women do in our culture. But some men do have trouble having orgasm from time to time, particularly in later years. It does not mean (as some men erroneously assume) that their sex lives are totally over.

That some females have more trouble having orgasm is probably highly influenced by conventional values and the traditional norms as well as the socialization process in growing up in a particular subculture in our culture. The woman's potentiality for having orgasm may or may not be developed by a given culture. Psychotheraphy and sex therapy of a philosophical nature can help both men and women integrate sex in their lives, including orgasm, in a more satisfactory way.

SUGGESTED FURTHER READING

Ard, Ben N., Jr. "Simultaneous Orgasm," *Marriage Counseling Quarterly,* 6 (1971), 30-32.

Ellis, Albert. "Is the Vaginal Orgasm a Myth?" *in* M. F. De Martino (Editor) *Sexual Behavior and Personality Characteristics* (New York: Citadel Press, 1963), pp. 348-360.

Lydon, Susan. "The Politics of Orgasms," *in* Robin Morgan (Editor) *Sisterhood Is Powerful* (New York: Vintage Books, 1970), pp. 197-205.

Marmor, Judd. "Some Considerations Concerning Orgasm in the Female," *in* M. F. De Martino (Editor) *Sexual Behavior and Personality Characteristics* (New York: Citadel Press, 1963), pp. 336-347.

Masters, William H., and Johnson, Virginia E. "Orgasm, Anatomy of the Female," *in* Albert Ellis and Albert Abarbanel (Editors) *The Encyclopedia of Sexual Behavior* New York: Hawthorne Books, 1961), pp. 788-793.

Stokes, Walter R. "Inadequacy of Female Orgasm as a Problem in Marriage Counseling,," *in* Ben N. Ard, Jr. & C. C. Ard (Editors) *Handbook of Marriage Counseling* (Palo Alto: Science & Behavior Books, 1969), pp. 360-367.

"Sexual activity, we see, is not merely a bald propagative act, nor, when propagation is put aside, is it merely the relief of distended vessels...It is the function by which all the finer activities of the organism, physical and psychic, may be developed and satisfied."

Havelock Ellis
On Life and Sex (1922, pp. 131-132)

CHAPTER 9

BIRTH CONTROL AND SAFER SEX

Attempts at birth control are as old as recorded history. As early as 3,000 B.C., primitive measures to prevent conception were used in Asia Minor. The earliest known recorded contraceptive formulas appeared on an Egyptian papyrus in 1850 B.C. Both formulas create an alkaline condition which scientists today recognize as spermicidal. It was not until the 1880's however that a modern method of birth control was made possible, when the diaphragm or pessary was devised.

Despite the fact that the diaphragm provides safe, effective, reliable birth control method, when correctly used, it posed problems for some women. Or, more accurately, some women caused themselves to have problems with this method through some of their irrational thinking.

I have had women clients who had irrational reasons for not liking to use the diaphragm. They did not like to touch themselves "down there," as they said, and therefore did not like having to insert the diaphragm in their vagina. Modern technology has invented plastic inserters, but obviously the problem is in how the woman thinks about herself and her genital organs.

The diaphragm has also posed other irrational problems for some women: to properly use the diaphragm, there must be some planning ahead; this necessitates facing consciously what one plans to do about sex in one's life, which is just what bothers some women. I have had women clients complain to me that the use of the diaphragm "interfered with lovemaking."

That is, they did not like having to interrupt their passionate lovemaking at the most inopportune time, to have to get up our of bed, go to the bathroom, and insert the diaphragm. Some of these women have taken so long to do this simple job that, by the time they return to the conjugal bed, their husband's erection (and perhaps even the inclination) are long gone.

When I have suggested that this problem has a very simple solution, namely putting the diaphragm in when the wife takes a shower in the afternoon before her husband's return from his day's work (or, for the working wife, when she takes her shower at night before going to bed), I have been told by a client that my suggestion of putting the diaphragm in early would "take all the spontaneity out of sex." Such a client might not want to admit, even to herself, that she actually wanted sex, or that she hoped her husband would make sexual overtures to her that night.

This case example shows how problems of birth control are related to sex and how a psychologist and marriage counselor might get involved in such matters. Since I am not physician, I do not get into the medical aspects of birth control with my clients. But as we shall see, sex (and one's attitudes, assumptions, and values regarding sex) frequently enter into the matter of birth control methods. It is with these matters that I as a psychologist and marriage counselor and sex therapist must deal.

My own case records, as well as those of marriage counselors throughout the country, implicate fear of pregnancy as a key factor in the breakdown of sexual pleasure and compatibility, and show that health is endangered by the consequent sexual dissatisfaction (Guttmacher, 1961, pp. 89-90). Fear of pregnancy, or possible pregnancy, can cause a woman to hold back from letting herself go in sexual intercourse and consequently interfere with her enjoyment of sex.

Some women I have had as clients have had orgasm problems because they held back from letting themselves go completely in sexual intercourse out of the *mistaken* belief that, if they do not have an orgasm, they cannot get pregnant. I have had to disabuse such women of this false idea and assure them that a woman can certainly get pregnant even if she does not have an orgasm in sexual intercourse. With the pill and all the other various birth control methods, there are many approaches to avoiding pregnancy that will not interfere with adequate sexual functioning and certainly will not interfere with having an orgasm.

In one research study it was found that more than two thirds of the women who failed at birth control had a basically unhealthy attitude toward sexual relationships and said they derived little or no pleasure from that aspect of their relationships (Guttmacher, 1961, p. 82). In this day of a wide variety of measures being available, it is a sad commentary on our society that a minority can keep the rest of the population in ignorance about adequate birth control methods. The majority of Americans are squarely behind proper instruction in birth control, and have been shown to be so in repeated surveys, over many years. But a minority, usually for religious reasons, has been opposed to birth control and able to influence legislatures, schools, and colleges so that it is difficult to teach preventive birth control methods, even today.

Because many teachers are afraid to teach scientific facts about birth control, many young people toady are using such inadequate methods as Saran Wrap and Coke douches (Ard, 1967, p. 102). We obviously need to put

138

all the scientific facts before the people and let each person decide whether or not he or she wants to use any birth control methods or not, and if so, which method. Such decisions cannot be well made in ignorance but must be based upon scientific evidence. Such scientific birth control knowledge needs to be instilled into most people's minds to offset the emotional rush of feelings likely to impede their rational decision-making process. For, after all, feelings are not tools of cognition.

The condom is frequently used by many couples before marriage and perhaps early in marriage but I, at least, seem to be hearing more complaints about the condom as a regular deice for continued use, particularly in view of the ready availability of better methods. For many people the disadvantages of the condom tend to outweigh its advantages. They complain that the condom dulls sensation by introducing an artificial membrane between the penis and the vagina. Also, rubber is a poor conductor of body warmth. Some wives have told me that they want to be able to feel their husbands's ejaculation.

One of the major problems centering around birth control methods and the decision to use them or not has been, in my practice at least, that of the definition of the role of the woman in the marriage and family life. I have had intelligent, college-educated women who knew all the latest birth control methods, and who even used them from time to time, but who arbitrarily defined their preordained role as being a mother (that is, having young babies to look after). Such women want to have a baby every few years to satisfy this limited and self-defeating definition of a woman. Birth giving is surely not the only role of a woman.

Both men and women in our culture have many irrational reactions when discussing birth control methods, whether or not to have children, how many, and what birth control methods would best enable them to have the sort of family they would like and which they could adequately take are of, emotionally and financially. Some couples go into marriage without even having heard each other out clearly with regard to their ability and desire to have children and how to rear them.

I recall in this connection one couple who came to see me who evidenced perhaps the clearest example of the man not hearing what the woman had told him about her not being able to have children. She had had a hysterectomy. This operation prevents a woman from ever having any children. The wife had carefully told her intended husband about her operation before she agreed to marry him. He had no objections at the time, but after they had been married several years they sought the professional services of a marriage counselor because, the husband said, he was concerned that they had had no children! When I checked with the husband in a private, individual session as to whether or not he had understood that his wife had had a hysterectomy prior to their marriage, he said yes. And yet he still wanted children and was unhappy with his wife because she had been "unable to conceive." In other words, he had heard the word *hysterectomy* but had not fully understood that his wife would never be able to have children. Such is the force of passion that it sometimes seems to cause partial deafness!

There are differences between the various social classes in their attitudes toward birth control. The lower classes tend to use "folk methods." Among the middle classes, effectiveness of contraceptive methods was found in one investigation to be related to positive and negative

140

feelings of husband or wife toward sexual relations (Gravatt, 1969, p. 251).

One of the most recent irrational responses to birth control has been the labeling of family planning (that is, birth control) as "genocide" by black militant males. These black men assume that the white population is trying to eliminate the black race through teaching black women birth control methods. Such paranoid ravings, rather than being dismissed as patently absurd, are sometimes believed by "liberals" who identify with the problems blacks are facing in this country and therefore accept without question whatever black militants happen to spout off about. When one investigates, however, one finds that, as a matter of fact, states, local agencies, and individuals served by them are guaranteed "freedom from coercion or pressure of mind or conscience" in deciding whether to participate in family planning programs (Gravatt, 1969, pp. 254-255). One also notes that is the black militant *males, with their machismo or stud concepts of masculinity, that holler "birth control is genocide," rather than the black women,* who have already had too many children by their own estimation and would like some means to prevent further pregnancies.

Irrational responses to birth control are many and varied (including even the bombing of family planning clinics). Some people get themselves into real emotional states about *other* peoples's decisions to use some form of birth control method. These are people who not only refuse to use any method themselves but who are even upset about anyone else using any. One young man I had as a client will perhaps serve to illustrate this sort of reaction.

This young man was in his senior year at a university and, prior to the time he was referred to me by the dean of students, had been making excellent progress in his studies and was soon to graduate with honors. He was well liked by his fellow students, enjoyed what seemed like a good social life, and had a great future ahead of him, according to his professors.

All of this changed drastically after he returned to campus from his Christmas vacation at home. He started cutting classes, failing to turn in his assignments, quit studying, began drinking excessively, carousing and, in the local parlance, "going to hell in a wheelbarrow." Such a radical change in behavior could hardly be missed by his friends and professors. He was about to fail in his studies and could possibly have been expelled from the university for some his extracurricular activities. So the dean referred the young man to me since I was at that time the university psychologist on the campus.

In our sessions it came out that he had heard some news at home during Christmas vacation that had radically altered his stance towards life. His father had taken him aside and told him that his mother had developed an illness recently and when they had visited the doctor he had suggested that she have no more children. Since this was a Polish family , they had all been Roman Catholics for as long as anyone could remember. A moral dilemma obviously presented itself at this point. The father and mother could have given up sex for the rest of their lives,. Or, they could have "left it in God's hand," as some people say, and done nothing to, prevent further pregnancies, taking their chances with the mother's life if she did get pregnant. If she did get pregnant and died as a result of the pregnancy, they would have said it was all "part of God's plan."

But the father told his son that he loved his wife and that they both had discussed the matter and had agreed to adopt some birth control method as the best possible solution under the circumstances. The son was shocked because this decision went against his church's teachings about birth control. And, he said, if one could decide to go against the church's teachings on this matter, then one could do the same thing on other matters. Then, he concluded, there was no point to life at all since there were no guidelines (nothing on which one could base one's life). Therefore he jumped to the conclusion that one might just as well live for the moment and he was, in effect, going to hell in a wheelbarrow.

This young man had made several serious errors in his thinking which led him to the false and self-defeating conclusions upon which he based his recent actions. He assumed that if the church was wrong on this matter of birth control then it might be wrong on other matters (a rational conclusion), and that if the way the church arrived at its moral positions was wrong then there were no ways one could arrive at reliable ethical guides to life (an unjustified conclusion which does not follow), and therefore he would follow no ethical rules whatsoever. Obviously this last conclusion was very self-defeating for this young man. In his psychotherapy (a deeply philosophical sort of psychotherapy) we went over carefully his thinking, his assumptions, and his conclusions, to help him rid himself of his twisted, faulty thinking, and to think through what he wanted to do with his life, even if others (his parents or the church) came to conclusions with which he did not agree.

There can be sound, reliable, logical and reasonable guides to action which have been arrived at without any of the assumptions the church makes. (Ard, *Rational Sex Ethics,* 1989) There are rational ethics available even for unbelievers. (White, 1948) Agnostics and atheists, as a matter of fact, do not go around robbing banks, raping women, and molesting little children, merely because they do not hold the supernatural presumptions held so unquestioningly by religious people. (Ard, *Living Without Guilt and/or Blame: Conscience, Superego and Psychotherapy,* 1983) Some people assume, like this young man, that religion is the only buttress of morals and that without religion there can be no basis for *any* ethical code. Without religion, people would just run amok, many persons (including my young client) believe. And that was just what he was doing, in effect.

But I persistently showed him where he evidently had made some mistakes in judgment, where it would be better to reexamine some of the assumptions he had made, and begin to question some of his premises. Through this fundamental reexamination of his recently adopted philosophy of life, he was able to see that he was literally doing himself in, so to speak. He came to see that perhaps his father and mother had every right to come to their conclusion to use some birth control methods; that his father valued his wife more than he valued the stance of the church on the question of birth control. This young man, through this deeply philosophical kind of psychotherapy, was also able to see that even if the church was wrong on this matter (and possibly others), that was insufficient reason for him to throw his own life down the drain.

Slowly, gradually, as we discussed his philosophy of life and challenged some of his previous irrational thinking, he began to see the effects of his wrongly arrived at conclusions. Then we began to delve into what he really wanted to do with his life, and he began to develop some more reasonable ideas about what it probably would be necessary for him to do if he wanted to realize some of the goals he desired. Some ethical actions would probably be necessary; he had better choose to finish college if he wanted to continue in the profession he was deeply interested in pursuing. When he realized that there are some values which logically follow from choosing life, even if one disagrees with the church about some of its moral positions, he began to take more rational control and responsibility for his life and the actions necessary for him to pursue to gain the goals he wanted. The decision to condone birth control can be a very ethical decision which leads to a better life.

The advent of the "pill" has forced many a person to reexamine their basic assumptions about sex in general and the role it may play as it is integrated into their lives. Having the pill as a birth control method has really liberated many women from merely being baby factories. The pill, however, has problems associated with it from a psychological point of view because of the necessity of planning ahead and taking the pill on a regular basis under the prescribed conditions (i. e., in other words, to be *accountable* for one's actions surrounding sex).

Some women clients of mine have trouble remembering to take the pill, and then they blame the pill when they get pregnant, when in fact there is nothing wrong with the pill, but merely their improper use of it. There are many reasons for one not remembering to take the pill. Some of the reasons may be rather hidden from view, so to speak; that is, a person may not be completely aware of why she "forgot" to take the pill. Psychologists, marriage counselors and sex therapists have techniques for helping their clients get at these hidden reasons.

Perhaps one of the biggest objections I have heard to birth control, other than the religious ones, is that it interferes with sex being "spontaneous" or unplanned. I see this objection in supposedly intelligent, well-educated people. One couple I encountered illustrated this attitude toward birth control. He was a medical student and she was enrolled in college nearby in another town. They usually were only able to see each other on weekends. She would ordinarily travel the short distance and they would stay at a motel together, usually having intercourse. They maintained this pattern for nearly three years without any birth control methods. They planned to be married in the future, after he graduated from medical school and had established himself. A pregnancy at this point in their live would be most inopportune, to say the least. And yet when I raised the question of what birth control methods they were using, she replied "none." When I asked why she said they wanted their lovemaking to be spontaneous and unplanned! She said she did not *plan* to have intercourse (although she admitted that they usually did when they spent the weekend in the motel). Sex in this view is something that just occurs spontaneously from time to time and just overwhelms people when they are swept away with passion! Therefore one does not have to face the fact that one has a sex life and had better plan for it as an integrated part of one's total life.

The pill in particular as a birth control method really must planned for; one needs to be aware of what day it is, when one last menstruated, and so on. The pill particularly must be decided upon long before the opportunity to have sex presents itself.

Another birth control method which is gaining in popularity among men is the vasectomy operation, which involves tying of the vas deferens so that sperm cannot get out of the scrotum. Many men are resorting to this means of birth control because they do not wish to have any more children. This operation is simpler for the male than the analogous one for the woman; that is, sterilization for the woman usually involves a more serious operation to tie off her tubes. This means going into the body under conditions which necessitate a hospital operating room, and so forth. The vasectomy operation can be performed in a physicians's office in a relatively much shorter time and no hospitalization is required. Only a local anesthetic is needed.

Many men have many irrational ideas to work through before they are ready for this operation. Some forms of this operation are irreversible, so the man has to be sure about his decision. But for the man who has already fathered all the children he thinks he can reasonably support, the vasectomy provides a simple, efficient, and good form of birth control.

Tying of the tubes or sterilization of the woman can be accomplished at the time of a Cesarean operation or at the normal birth of the last child a couple feel they can afford. This is a permanent form of birth control and, once again, irreversible.

Medical reasons, certain diseases, and other considerations might lead one to consider these means of birth control. They should be thoroughly discussed between the partners and with competent medical consultation before arriving at such decisions. Psychologists, marriage counselors and sex therapists frequently get into discussions of the pros and cons of various birth control methods (not from the medical aspects) but from examining with the clients what are the various alternatives open to them in planning to integrate sex in their lives in a rational manner.

Where none of the birth control methods such as the pill, the condom, the diaphragm, intrauterine devices, and so forth have been properly used, then abortion may be still another alternative. It *can* be considered a form of birth control, but we shall discuss it in a separate chapter.

SUGGESTED FURTHER READING

Ard, Ben N., Jr. "The Sex Hypocrisy of Adults, *Sexology,* 32 (1965), pp.292-294.

Ard, Ben N., Jr. "Gray Hair for the Teenage Father," pp. 95-104, in Farber, Seymour M. & Wilson, Roger H. L. (Editors) *Teenage Marriage and Divorce.* Berkeley: Diablo Press, 1967.

Ard, Ben N., Jr. *Living Without Guilt and/or Blame: Conscience, Superego and Psychotherapy.* Smithtown, N.Y.: Exposition Press, 1983.

Ard, Ben Neal, Jr. *Rational Sex Ethics.* New York: Peter Lang, 2nd ed., 1989.

Bronowski, J. *Science and Human Values.* New York: Harper Torchbooks, 1956.

Cisler, Lucinda. "Unfinished Business: Birth Control and Women's Liberation," pp. 245-289, *in* Morgan, Robin (Editor) *Sisterhood is Powerful.* New York: Vintage Books, 1970.

Gravatt, Arthur E. "Family Planning," pp. 243-279, *in* Broderick, C. B. & Bernard, Jessie (Editors) *The Individual, Sex and Society.* Baltimore: John Hopkins Press, 1969.

Guttmacher, A. F. *The Complete Book of Birth Control.* New York: Ballantine Books, 1961.

Himes, Norman E. & Stone, Abraham. *Practical Birth Control Methods.* New York: Viking Press, 1938.

Hoffman, R. Joseph & Larue, Gerald A. *Biblical v Secular Ethics: The Conflict.* Buffalo: Prometheus Books, 1988.

Kirkendall, Lester A. "A Counselor Looks at Contraceptives for the Unmarried," pp. 264-278, *in* Ard, Ben N., Jr. & Ard, C. C. (Editors) *Handbook of Marriage Counseling.* Palo Alto: Science & Behavior Books, 1969.

Nielsen, Kai. *Ethics Without God.* Buffalo: Prometheus Books, 1973.

Otto, Max. *Science and the Moral Life.* New York: The New American Library, 1949.

Rainwater, L., & Weinstein, K. K. *And the Poor Get Children.* Chicago: Quadrangle Books, 1960.

Sanger, Margaret. *My Fight for Birth Control.* New York Farrar & Rinehart, 1931.

Sperry, Roger. *Science and Moral Priority: Merging Mind, Brain, and Human Vales.* New York: Columbia University Press, 1983.

White, Amber Blanco. *Ethics for Unbelievers.* London: Routledge & Kegan Paul, 1948.

"It was as part of its comprehensive attempt to make the sexual act as difficult as possible that the Church devised laws against the practice of abortion."

G. Rattray Taylor
Sex in History   (1954, p. 58)

CHAPTER 10

ABORTION: A RATIONAL ALTERNATIVE

When couples have sexual intercourse without taking proper precautions through reliable, scientific birth control methods, they may ultimately be faced with a problem of whether or not to consider abortion. There are significant changes taking place in the public's attitude toward abortion in recent years.

Mankind throughout the ages has used abortion, but until rather recently in our culture it was not openly considered as a possible or reasonable choice. Abortion was illegal and a black-market, back-alley, undercover sort of thing. Abortion was not rationally considered as a legitimate alternative for many years in our culture. In these previous years it was practically synonymous with "criminal" abortion and the "therapeutic" (noncriminal) type was rarely discussed in public.

Some people assumed that married people should "accept what babies the good Lord sent" and that single girls who got pregnant as a result of having "illicit" premarital sex would be the only ones who ever wanted abortions. Therefore, according to this line of "thought," abortions should be illegal and criminally prosecuted. The fact that many women died from these illegal abortions, performed under unantiseptic conditions, frequently by unqualified people, was considered only "just desserts," since these "bad" single girls who were having all that illicit fun should "pay" for it!

But the facts have indicated for a long time that many married women, with too many children already, have wanted to have abortions.

The law has forced such eminently respectable women to risk their lives with back-street quacks because the law for so many years did not recognize the right to abortion. Countless studies have shown that, contrary to public notions on the subject, induced abortion is primarily a problem of the overburdened married woman rather than of unmarried women of supposed "loose moral standards." (Himes and Stone, 1938, p. 159)

There has been some progress in recent years with regard to the right to abortion. Despite the fact that some people have religious and moral objections to it, and have been active in preventing others, who do not share the same religious or moral assumptions, from their right to abortion, some progress has been made in considering the practice in a more rational manner. Those people who do not approve of abortion simply do not have to avail themselves of it; and they do not need the law to support the moral principles which interfere with other people's different ethical beliefs. The arbitrary defining of any abortion as "murder" (as some moralistic people see it) need not limit the freedom of those who do not view abortion in this light.

A significant percentage of unwanted children born to mothers who have been refused the right to abortion develop psychiatric instability, according to the Committee on Psychiatry and Law of the Group for the Advancement of Psychiatry (1970, p. 11). The same group, after studying the problem at length, recommended that abortion, when performed by a licensed physician, be entirely removed from the domain of criminal law. (Group for the Advancement of Psychiatry, 1970, p. 49) I would concur with their belief that a woman should have the right to an abortion or not, just as she has the right to marry or not.

The American Civil Liberties Union has also defended the rights of women to have an abortion. The ACLU believes that all criminal sanctions should be removed from the performance of an abortion, and that the laws and standards governing this medical procedure be the same as those which govern the performance of all medical procedures. (Group for the Advancement of Psychiatry, 1970, p. 27) The ACLU argues that present abortion laws (that is, those which make it illegal) infringes upon the constitutional rights of women to decide whether and when to have a child. The criminal sanctions against abortion also deprive women of their lives and liberty, in the sense of deciding how their bodies are to be used. (Group for the Advancement of Psychiatry, 1970, p. 28)

Still another national organization, the National Council on Family Relations, has published a position paper on abortion (1971), in which it is clearly stated that, while the NCFR supports family planning education as a preventive approach, it also strongly endorses the repeal of all laws which prohibit safe medical abortion in this country. (National Council on Family Relations, 1971, p. 401) It further recommends that abortion be the legal right of all women and a private matter between a woman and her physician. (National Council on Family Relations, 1971, p. 401)

These national organizations represent an increasing number of people who believe that abortion is a legitimate alternative which should be available to all women. That is, every woman should have the right to decide for herself whether or not she wishes to have an abortion. This point of view is gaining adherents and will probably predominate in the future. However, there are still lots of people who think abortion is "murder" and a grievous sin. Some such people feel so self-righteous and absolutely certain about their "moral" position that they proceed to bomb clinics where abortions are performed!

I still see clients who are troubled about whether or not to have an abortion. One twenty-four-year-old woman from the East Coast had discovered that what she assumed would never happen to her had, indeed, happened: she became pregnant in circumstances where marriage to the father of her child-to-be was not a possibility. He was already married, she discovered, when she told him about the pregnancy.

Her parents were not very mature adults and they handled the situation rather badly. They first insisted that she have an abortion. She refused. Then her parents put her on a plane to San Francisco (with a one-way ticket, yet) and told her that they did not want to see her again until she had "gotten rid of it." The young woman had a very bad time during her pregnancy; she was often hysterical and sometimes denied that she was pregnant. But denying her pregnancy did not make it go away; this defense mechanism, like so many others, is useless in resolving the problem.

Since she insisted for too long a time that she would prefer to have the baby, she was referred to the Florence Crittenton Home, where the birth occurred. Fortunately, the parents were persuaded to seek some professional help on their own and began to make the needed changes in their own attitudes. Their initial position on abortion and their later sending their pregnant daughter away to have the baby were based on their fear of what neighbors would think of them. The young woman finally decided to give her baby up for adoption. But if she had had some psychotherapy earlier, or had a better sex education before she ever got pregnant, she might not have had to undergo this ordeal as she did.

Abortion is a legitimate alternative and had better be considered as such. This young woman would have been much better off had she had an abortion rather than carrying her baby to full term, giving birth to it, and then giving it up for adoption.

Perhaps some of the actual thinking of such clients will serve to show what is involved in this sort of problem. In what follows, some responses of both the client and the therapist will be given. This young woman client has just reported that she is pregnant.

Client: *Well, I never thought it would happen to me but it has.*

Therapist: *What have you considered doing about this situation?*

Client: *My parents wanted me to get an abortion.*

Therapist: *What do you want to do?*

Client: *I think abortion is a horrible idea!*

Therapist: *Why?*

Client: *Well, it's practically murder.*

Therapist: *Who says?*

Client: *Lots of people do. Haven't you heard that?*

Therapist: *Yes, I've heard that some people believe any abortion is ipso facto a murder, but that is hardly reason enough for one deciding that abortion is murder. A lot of people have all sorts of unfounded assumptions about abortion. Such ideas had better be checked logically and scientifically and not just swallowed whole. Have you checked out your ideas with any reliable, scientific authority?*

Client: I have talked with some of my friends...

Therapist: Are they qualified enough to have a competent opinion?

Client: Well, isn't anyone entitled to their opinion?

Therapist: Only in a very loose, sloppy sense. When it comes to scientific matters, the man on the street, or your old maid aunt, or old wives' tales are rather poor sources of reliable opinion. Have you discussed abortion with a competent physician who has had experience in performing these operations?

Client: No.

Therapist: Some people assume that an abortion is a very dangerous operation, that it frequently can prevent a woman from ever having any more children, and many other sorts of scary things. Have you picked up any such notions?

Client: Yes, one of my girl friends told me sterility can result from an abortion. Isn't that so?

Therapist: It could possibly happen and perhaps has happened, but more usually only where such operations are performed in a back alley by incompetent people. It is also interesting to note that frequently some of the sterility probably already existed prior to the operation and therefore was falsely attributed to the abortion. But don't take my word for it, check it out   *with a competent physician who has had experience performing many such operations under proper conditions. Then your opinion about abortions would be based upon* scientific opinion and facts rather than upon rumors and back-street gossip and old wives' tales. Are you willing to take the time to check it out?

Client: Well... I don't know. I just feel it is wrong...

Therapist: But feelings *are insufficient to determine such an important decision in your life. What you need more than feelings are <u>facts</u>. And some clear thinking about what your basic values are. You will have to think straight on this issue if you want to arrive at a rational conclusion.*

Client: *But I'm scared...*

Therapist: *I can understand that but you would not avoid going to a dentist merely because you were scared, would you?*

Client: *(laughing) I guess I have done that, too. But I see what you mean.*

Therapist: *I'll give you three names of competent physicians to consult and you can take your choice.*

This excerpt from a session with a client concerned about abortion shows how necessary it is for women to think very carefully through their basic values, their assumptions, and to develop a philosophy of life that enables them to take the responsibility for their own lives and their bodies. Each woman has to decide for herself whether or not she has the right to limit her own reproduction. If she believes she has that right, then she has the right to obtain an abortion under appropriate conditions and circumstances. I think the day when a woman can irresponsibly go on having too many children, even when she is not able to take proper care of them, is fast drawing to a close. The population explosion has forced many people to rethink their position about birth control; and abortion too will probably soon take its place among the legitimate alternatives open to pregnant women.

Several states (California, Colorado, Hawaii, and New York, for example) have liberalized their laws regarding abortion to various degrees. As more women realize their rights, presumably more states will pass such laws and even some of the above states may liberalize their present laws. Many famous women who have had abortions recently placed an ad listing that fact in one of the mass media publications; such a statement would have been unthinkable not too many years ago. The times, they are achangin', indeed, both in song and reality.

I have had women clients who had a problem regarding abortion which might be termed "after the fact." That is, some women who have let a man talk them into have an abortion as a result of a premarital pregnancy, have then felt so guilty about going through with it that they have come into my office and discussed whether or not to tell their new boyfriend that they had had an abortion. This attitude toward the procedure practically classifies abortion as a shameful thing. Some of my clients have said that they hated to admit having an abortion to their prospective husbands because they assumed that the men would turn away from them in rejection.

Some women feel the same way about premarital pregnancy even when they carry the baby to term, have it, and then give it up for adoption. I have had clients who wonder whether or not to tell their prospective husbands about previously having had a child out of wedlock and giving it up for adoption. It would seem that such women judge themselves as losing, whether they have the baby or have an abortion. I see no justifiable reason why women should be blamed because they have had an abortion or a child out of wedlock, and given the baby up for adoption. It may have been an unfortunate event that they got pregnant and had to decide on adoption or abortion, but they are no less worthwhile as a person merely because they may have decided they made a mistake. Abortions are a legitimate alternative, whether one is married or not, and no woman should feel guilty merely because she has had an abortion. (Ard, 1983, 1989)

In the research done on induced abortion by Gebhard, *et al* (1958, p. 192), they reported that, for their own sample,

"... *we find that the great percentage of the women who have had an illegal abortion stated that it had been the best solution to their immediate problem. This widespread difference between our overt culture as expressed in our laws and public announcements and our convert culture as expressed in what people actually do and secretly think is as true with abortion as with most types of sexual behavior.*"

Some so-called authorities in the field have been more troublesome than helpful because they have stressed the "bad" consequences of induced abortion to the point where they have unnecessarily frightened women away from it. As Gebhard *et al* (1958, pp. 203-204) have pointed out, "Usually the unfavorable sequelae of abortion are emphasized as a means of frightening persons from having premarital intercourse, just as are the horrors of venereal disease."

Some psychiatrists have given rather exaggerated warnings about

164

depression following induced abortions. Yet, in the research of Gebhard *et al* (1958, p. 208), less than 10 percent of the females in their sample reported psychological upset over their induced abortions. In my experience it is not the abortion per se that causes the depression that sometimes has followed but rather the guilt feelings which result from unquestioned value assumptions. Where the woman is willing to reexamine and challenge her unquestioned assumptions and premises, she can come to see abortion as a sometimes necessary step and thus eliminate any guilt feelings. (Ard, 1983) Depression does not usually follow abortion and it need not necessarily continue if the woman is willing to work on her irrational ideas which cause the depression. If a woman has any second thoughts that are self-defeating, she may wish to examine them carefully with a professional person in a helping relationship where she can rigorously reexamine her previously unquestioned premises and assumptions and get rid of those that are detrimental.

SUGGESTED FURTHER READING

Abortion: Murder or Mercy? As told to Margaret Witte Moore (Greenwich, Conn.: Gold Medal Books, 1962).

Ard, Ben N., Jr. *Living Without Guilt and/or Blame: Conscience, Superego and Psychotherapy* (Smithtown, N.Y.: Exposition Press, 1983).

Ard, Ben Neal, Jr. *Rational Sex Ethics* (New York: Peter Lang, 1989).

Cisler, Lucinda. "Unfinished Business: Birth Control and Women's Liberation," *in* Robin Morgan (Editor) *Sisterhood Is powerful* (New York: Vintage Books, 1970), pp. 245-289.

Gebhard, Paul H., *et al. Pregnancy, Birth, and Abortion* (New York: Harper, 1958).

Group for the Advancement of Psychiatry. *The Right to Abortion: A Psychiatric View* (New York: Charles Scribner's Sons, 1970).

Guttmacher, Alan F. "Miscarriages and Abortions," *in* Morris Fishbein and Ernest W. Burgess (Editors) *Successful Marriage* (Garden City, N.Y.: Doubleday, revised edition, 1963).

Himes, Norman E., and Stone, Abraham. *Practical Birth Control Methods* (New York: Viking Press, 1938).

Neumann, Gottfried. "Abortion," *in* Albert Ellis and Albert Abarbanel
(Editors) *The Encyclopedia of Sexual Behavior* (New York:
Hawthorne Books, 1961), pp. 35-43.

National Council on Family Relations. "Position Paper on Abortion," *The
Family Coordinator*, 20 (1971), 401-402.

"The first thing that women say when a man who loves them becomes jealous is that there is no cause for jealousy, that it is the outcome of "unwarranted anxiety of losing his dearest"; and they are right. For if the jealousy is justified, why should there be any anxiety? If it be justified, everything is over, and there is nothing more to fear. The dread of losing one's dearest possession when one has already lost it, is an silly as it would be to fear death when one is already dead. Consequently there is no such thing as warrantable jealousy."

Bernhard A. Bauer

Woman and Love (1927, Vol. 1, p. 232)

CHAPTER 11

JEALOUSY: INEVITABLE OR ELIMINATABLE?

In the whole field of sex relations between human beings, one of the most explosive and difficult problems to handle is that of jealousy. Murders have been committed in a jealous rage. Many beatings have been administered and endured because of jealousy. Untold scenes, sleepless nights, quarrels, and fights have occurred over jealous feelings. Many friendships and love relationships as well as marriages have been terminated because of it.

Obviously jealousy means different things to different people. It includes feelings, attitudes, assumptions, thoughts, definitions (frequently highly arbitrary), and a wide variety of behaviors. A person can be said to be jealous when he or she is intolerant of rivalry (real or assumed), or unfaithfulness (or even suspected unfaithfulness), and hence apprehensiveness about the possible loss of another's devotion. One can be said to be jealous when he or she is distrustfully watchful, suspicious, or shows zealous vigilance regarding his or her sexual partner.

Some people assume that jealousy is a sign of love; that if one is not jealous then he or she is not in love (according to this particular theory). But this assumption is just one of many about jealousy that had better be seriously examined and questioned. It is a grave error to assume that jealousy is a sign of real or true love.

Many people assume that jealousy is a natural, normal, innate phenomenon, and may be expected to occur in all relationships (particularly where sex is involved), that is, among lovers or spouses. Such is simply not the case, however.

A cross-cultural study of sexual relations between men and women, both in and outside of marriage, will show that most of the reactions which can be categorized as jealous are culturally determined and not innate. The well-known hospitality of Eskimo husbands, who share their wives with visiting males, is a case in point. Further proof may be seen in the fact that jealousy does not occur among the Lesu (Powdermaker, 1983), where gifts are made to women with whom intercourse is secured, and the women turn these gifts over to their husbands.

In fact, jealousy is essentially an *irrational* reaction, frequently infantile as well as paranoid. Jealousy is thus the expression of a weak, if not sick, personality. Projection of one's extramarital desires upon one's partner to avoid admitting one's own feet of clay is a very frequent occurrence among jealous spouses.

If a person has had a very deprived childhood and might be said to be starved for love, he or she may become so dependent upon the spouse that the slightest expression of any interest whatsoever of the mate in anyone else is taken as a dire threat to one's very existence. It seems that too many people assume that they always have to have the constant and complete and exclusive love and attention of their partners or else it is a catastrophe.

These ideas are irrational and can obviously be very self-defeating and cause many problems among both the married and the unmarried. Such irrational ideas need not be allowed to ruin one's life; they can be challenged, questioned, and eliminated, although it may take rather extensive marriage counseling or psychotherapy to accomplish this task.

Some spouses often try to "test" the love of their partners and thus provoke jealous reactions. They sometimes even go so far as to assume that if there is no jealous reaction to their "harmless flirting," for example, the spouse must not love them anymore. The obvious self-defeating nature of such behavior often escapes such people and may only be realized when pointed out in a marriage counseling or psychotherapy session. Sometimes group sessions with married couples are helpful in getting individuals to see more clearly just what they are doing. The fact that other men and women in the group agree about their behavior makes it somewhat stronger than an opinion coming from their therapist alone.

Too many couples get married and live many years together without ever spelling out just exactly what their expectations of each other are and just what specific behaviors with the other sex are acceptable and which are off limits for that particular couple. This understanding would have better been reached long before marriage but such matters are frequently not clarified even after many quarrels and innumerable fights. During courtship, couples could consider signs of jealousy as danger signals rather than signs of love. If they cannot work out their expectations of each other before they are married, it may prove even more difficult afterward, since the rules tend to tighten up after marriage. A man may permit his girl friend to dance with another man many times without saying much, but after marriage he may lay down the law in no uncertain terms, even to the point of breaking her jaw.

Jealousy would not arise as easily if men and women could gain a clearer understanding of sex and sexual relations. For example, there is fairly clear evidence that men are not monogamous by nature. A wife who understands this will not expect her husband to automatically become blind to other women's charms merely because he is now married. Likewise, a wife can rave about the good looks of a particular movie star or a man she sees at a party without necessarily having to break up her marriage. Husbands had better realize this.

If fear of unfaithfulness is the issue, then what causes the possibility of unfaithfulness needs to be understood. Unfulfilled sexual desires can be one of the main causes of unfaithfulness in both sexes. However, the wife who realizes this and acts accordingly need have few worries. One such wife said, "I make sure that he has plenty of sex at home, then I don't have to worry about him when he is away from home." This philosophy will go a long way toward solving a basic part of the problem, although in some cases it may not be the complete solution, since other factors may also be involved.

The desire for variety and new contacts seems to be more strongly evidenced in men than in women in our culture. What is done about the "rules of the game" (and particularly regarding extramarital affairs) needs to be worked out by each couple. It can be done fairly, sensibly, and ethically as well as with allowances made for individual differences. (Ard, 1989)

Where there is a real commitment between two spouses, jealous possessiveness is unnecessary and uncalled for, to say the least. Trust rather than mistrust must of necessity be the basic ingredient in a healthy marriage. Where there can be no trust, separation and divorce seem more indicated than a life filled with jealousy, accusations, recriminations, or constant checking on the partner.

We in our culture encourage jealousy by rearing people to believe that it is more important for them to *be loved* than to *love.* In our culture, unfortunately, too many spouses view their mates as, in effect, their property, a possession, rather than as an independent human being. Naturally with this kind of upbringing we have an enormous amount of jealousy in marital relations as well as in premarital ones. (Clanton & Smith, *Jealousy*, 1986)

When an individual notes jealousy within himself, there are at least two ways to get rid of it. He can check out the facts, for one things. When a man comes home unexpectedly and sees his wife kissing a stranger (at least to him), before he attacks the man and his own wife with gun or knife, it would be better if he tries to find out who the strange man is and what are the circumstances. The man might just be the wife's long-lost brother or Uncle Joe just back from Africa. Second, if, after checking, one finds that one's spouse is involved with another person, he or she then has to choices: divorce or learning to live with that fact. Neither has to have jealousy as part of the package. If jealousy continues, perhaps the person had better turn to some professional help in the form of marriage counseling or psychotherapy to get at the underlying assumptions and remove them. Jealousy is not necessarily inevitable. (Ard, *in* Clanton & Smith, 1986, pp. 166-169)

Proof of the fact that jealousy is essentially a sick reaction is found in Abraham Maslow's study of self-actualizing people (that is, psychologically healthy or mature individuals): among such people he found the absence of jealousy. (Maslow, 1970, p. 195) So healthy people are apparently not overcome by jealousy. One has jealous feelings because of essentially self-defeating things one tells oneself about the possibilities of his or her partner having sexual relations with another and leaving the marital bed as a result. There are better ways of handling these feelings than giving in to them. One can challenge, question, and get rid of these self-defeating assumptions and live, thereby, a more joyful, trusting, and satisfying life, without jealousy.

What one *assumes* in matters of jealousy frequently determines what actions will be taken and possibly what consequences will result. If one assumes that jealousy is a natural, normal, inevitable and justified response to a given situation, that will lead to certain actions and consequences. If, however, jealousy is seen as not always justified or even normal, then different reactions can be expected.

In looking at jealous reactions among men and women, obviously it makes some difference whether the man and woman are married, engaged, going "steady," or just casually dating. The varying degrees of intimacy involve varying degrees of commitment and responsibility (or accountability), implicit as well as explicit. Different people assume different things at each of these stages of commitment and therefore *define* behavior accordingly. It is these differences in what is considered acceptable behavior on the part of one's partner that frequently causes difficulty.

When one is dating casually, one may not like one's date to pay too much attention to others while on the date, but usually he or she does not feel entirely justified in making too much an issue about it, since the obligations are fairly limited here. As one moves through steady dating into engagement and marriage, however, the limits of acceptable behavior frequently narrow down considerably. Many of the difficulties that arise around jealous reactions could possibly be reduced if couples were more explicit about what their expectations are for each other as they move through these various stages of commitment. What was acceptable during casual dating may not be equally acceptable during engagement or marriage.

Certainly by the time marriage is contemplated, a certain basic trust would seem to be required. If marriage partners cannot trust each other, there is little hope for the future of the marriage. Partners who are really committed to each other should not have to (or feel the need to) continually check up on each other.

As an illustration of how one's assumptions influence one's behavior, consider the man or woman who assumes that unless his or her partner shows some jealousy now and then, it follows (in his or her mind) that the partner does not love the other. Obviously this kind of assumption can lead to all sorts of self-defeating behavior. It would hardly seem to be a justifiable assumption to make.

One man, known to me in my practice as a marriage counselor, was always very proud of his beautiful wife. When he was out of town (which was frequent since he was a railroad engineer), he never objected when his wife went out to dinner and dances with men friends of theirs. He always said that he trusted his wife completely. Did this mean (since he wasn't jealous) that he did not love her? Not at all. He just defined acceptable behavior on the part of his wife in broader ways, perhaps, than other men might.

Other clients of mine have said, "I don't mind my spouse dancing, kissing or petting with others, as long as he (or she) comes home to me at night. I want to be the one he (or she) sleeps with." Each person would probably draw the line of acceptable behavior for his partner at a different place. There are no absolutes here, in the sense of universally agreed upon limits. Reading some cultural anthropology is a good antidote for anyone who believes otherwise.

But what is important for each couple, if they are to avoid unpleasant jealous reactions, is that they each spell out in explicit detail just what their assumptions and requirements as to the limits of acceptable behavior are. This had better be done early in the game rather than late. Too often one merely assumes that the other agrees, without ever checking it out. Then when the behavior reveals the underlying (but unspoken) assumptions, all hell frequently breaks loose. People have been beaten up, shot, and killed because of just these unspoken assumptions and the resulting jealous reactions. It might not be a bad idea to discuss possible hypothetical situations ahead of time, just to ascertain each other's expectations.

Checking out one' assumptions regarding acceptable behavior on the part of one's partner in unforseen situations is probably one of the best ways to avoid later unfortunate actions of a jealous sort, which one might regret. Easy ways to discuss such possible situations are after seeing movies, TV shows, reading novels, or even observing other people's behavior at cocktail parties where, perhaps, some hanky-panky is observed in the kitchen. Talk it over first while it is *other* people's behavior, since it is usually easier to be calmer about their behavior than one's own partner's, if one is emotionally involved with that partner.

Another illustration of how one's assumptions can get one into trouble as far as jealous reactions are concerned occurs when a husband looks approvingly at some woman other than his wife and his wife "catches him at it." Often the wife assumes that her husband would like to have sexual relations with the other woman (she might be right, on occasion); she then assumes that he must not love her anymore (not necessarily true since he probably did not go blind when he got married). She may assume that "all men are polygamous by nature" (she might be close to the truth here), and that therefore no man can be trusted (a mistaken assumption that can lead to real trouble in a marriage). It is a common assumption in our culture that it is just as bad a "sin" to lust after another man's wife (even if you don't do anything about it!) as it is to actually commit adultery. Yet this very assumption leads to self-blame and blaming one's spouse, neither of which is very helpful to maintaining good relations in a marriage.

What provokes jealousy and is seen therefore as a threat to a relationship varies from couple to couple. All sorts of behavior may occur which one set of partners would never consider a threat to their relationship, while another couple would immediately break up their relationship at the first occurrence of even one instance of such behavior. And such behaviors range all the way from flirting through kissing, necking, petting, and even including sexual intercourse with someone other than one's partner.

Where you draw the line is not as important to the stability of your relationship as is the explicit communication of your underlying values, assumptions, and expectations. It is much easier to spell out these things before situations arise that arouse your emotions.

Perhaps choosing hypothetical situations to initiate discussion will assist you in discovering what self-defeating assumptions you are harboring.

By checking out these expectations and assumptions with you partner ahead of time, you can reduce the instances which might call forth jealous reactions and eventuate in actions that cannot be retracted.

It would seem to be easier to trust one's partner when one has established the mutually agreed upon limits, the rules of the game in this particular relationship, and one's basic values, before stressful situations arise, along with escalating emotions. And trust is a better base for a marriage than jealousy, any time.

SUGGESTED FURTHER READING

Ard, Ben N., Jr. "How to Avoid Destructive Jealousy," *Sexology*, 34 (1967), 356-348.

Ard, Ben N., Jr. "How Jealousy Ruins Sex," *Sexology*, 37 (1971), 28-30.

Ard, Ben N., Jr. "Avoiding Destructive Jealousy," *in* Clanton, Gordon & Smith, Lynn G. (Editors) *Jealousy* (Lanham: University Press of America, 1986), pp. 166-169.

Bohm, Edward. "Jealousy," *in* Ellis, Albert & Abarbanel, Albert (Editors) *The Encyclopedia of Sexual Behavior* (New York: Hawthorn Books, 1961), pp. 567-574.

Clanton, Gordon & Smith, Lynn G. (Editors) *Jealousy* (Lanham: University Press of America, 1986).

Ellis, Albert. "Jealousy," *in* Ellis, Albert. *The American Sexual Tragedy* (New York: Twayne, 1954), pp. 122-138.

Maslow, A. H. *Motivation and Personality* (New York: Harper & Row, 2nd Edition, 1970).

180

Mead, Margaret. "Jealousy: Primitive and Civilized," *in* Schmalhausen, Samuel D. & Calverton, V. F. (Editors) *Woman's Coming of Age* (New York: Liveright, 1931), pp. 35-48.

Powdermake, Hortense. *Life in Lesu* (New York: Norton, 1932).

"Almost the entire history of mankind demonstrates that man is not, biologically, a truly monogamous animal; that he tends to be more monogynous than monogamic, desiring one woman at a time rather than a single woman for a lifetime, and that even when he acts monogynously he craves strongly occasional adulterous affairs in addition to his regular marital sex. The female of the human species seems to be less strongly motivated toward plural sexuality than is the male; but she, too, when she can have varietistic outlets with social impunity, quite frequently takes advantage of them."

Albert Ellis (*in* Gerhard
Neubeck (Editor) *Extra-marital
Relations,* 1969, p. 154)

CHAPTER 12

EXTRAMARITAL SEX: TO "SWING" OR
NOT TO "SWING"

Many people assume that extramarital sex relations are the major
cause of divorce; certainly many marriages are "on the rocks" because of
them. One's basic assumptions about human motivation come to light when
extramarital relations are discussed. Many of my clients are troubled by
such relations, either accomplished, suspected, or desired.

Many women in our culture have some assumptions about men and
extramarital relations that need careful examination. There is the common
assumption, for example, that no matter how well a woman treats a man, or
how "good" the man is (or intends to be), he *will* be unfaithful to his wife
or girl friend *sooner or later.* Now there are some statistical probabilities
involved which arise out of the scientific research done in this area. And
the probabilities are that *many* men and women *do* get involved in
extramarital relations. But *not all men,* nor certainly *not all women,* are
involved in them.

What are the reasons for extramarital relations? As Albert Ellis
(1969) has shown, there are both *healthy* and *disturbed* reasons for having
them. Some of the healthy reasons are sexual varietism, love enhancement,
experiential drives, adventure seeking, sexual curiosity, social and cultural
inducements, and sexual deprivation. Some of the disturbed reasons are low
frustration tolerance, hostility to one's spouse, self-depreciation, ego-
bolstering, escapism in general as well as marital escapism, various sexual

disturbances, and so-called "excitement needs."

Sexual varietism is just a natural desire for some variety in one's sexual life. This varies in different individuals, of course, and the degree of the desire for sexual variety may not be very strong in some people and quite strong in others. It is important to recognize this factor as a normal, natural, healthy one rather than prematurely assuming that it is a sign of disturbance.

Love enhancement may be considered a normal, natural desire to enhance one's love life, which usually, ultimately, results in some sexual experience if the love relationships develop to their normal conclusion. According to some authorities (Ellis, 1969, p. 154), "Healthy human beings are generally capable of loving pluralistically, on both a serial and a simultaneous basis." I suppose one of the questions I am most often faced with from clients in marriage counseling is "Can a person love more than one person at a time?" The answer seems to be yes, one can love more than one member of the other sex at the same time, or more accurately, during the same period in one's life. In other words, maybe not at the same moment but certainly during the same period of time. Scheduling becomes a problem, usually, as well as whether or not the partners involved know about each other in particular.

The question of whether or not extramarital relations reflect back love enhancement on the marriage relationship is often claimed. It is possible and has, evidently, occurred in some instances.

Experiential drives are the desire to savor a variety of experiences. These are ordinarily considered natural and normal when it comes to books, or wines, for example, but many people would draw the line when it comes to extramarital relations. Some people, however, do manage to experience a variety of sexual experiences throughout their lives.

Adventure seeking is closely related. Some people like to take a boat through raging rapids rather than a train along the riverside. That sort of thing may not be extremely common but it is understandable to many who perhaps do not have the urge themselves. The same cannot be said when it comes to sexual adventuring; many people in our culture object strenuously to any sexual adventuring, particularly when it involves extramarital relations. But the thrill of the chase is not limited to African safaris.

Sexual curiosity is also a natural, normal part of human behavior. It helps explain why men have frequently sought out the native girls in whatever clime. Stereotypes are overcome in this manner, which cannot be all bad. Men and women manage to overcome language barriers and communicate sufficiently well to have sexual relations all over the world. Wondering whether or not the grass is greener on the over side of the fence is an age-old preoccupation which still figures in some human relations, particularly extramarital relations. Men and women do make love in essentially the same fashion the world over but the nuances still cause the sexes to seek each other out, for better or worse. Some individuals may have extramarital in order to bring new sex techniques back into the marital sexual relationship. I have had women clients who never had an orgasm with their husbands and consequently tried an extramarital affair so, they said, they might have had at least one experience of orgasm.

Social and cultural inducements cause some people to have extramarital sex. In the business world, some wives have granted sexual favors to their husband's bosses in order to help their husbands advance in the organization. Some husbands have even suggested such maneuvers to their wives. These instances may not represent the healthiest kind of sexual behavior, but there are many social and cultural inducements toward extramarital sex which fall within the normal range, that is, the people do not consider the inducements abnormal.

I have had clients who have reported to me that, when their spouses were not available for considerable periods of time, members of the other sex have offered to "pinch hit" and substitute for the temporarily missing bed partner. Men who are serving overseas for three or four years frequently have reported that there were many social and cultural inducements to have extramarital sex.

Sexual deprivation of course is an obvious reason for seeing extramarital relations. Some have falsely claimed to be sexual deprived in order to justify their extramarital affairs. But I have heard a woman in therapy tell her mate in my presence to get his sex elsewhere and not bother her about sex anymore. When such a husband decides to get his sexual desires satisfied elsewhere, it certainly would seem to be understandable, although there can be neurotic problems which become involved in this sort of case.

Among the many disturbed reasons for extramarital relations, low frustration tolerance is a very frequent one. When sexual problems arise in marriage, some individuals have such a low frustration tolerance that they immediately turn elsewhere for sexual satisfaction. They might better take the time to try to work out their sexual problems themselves or to seek out professional help in resolving some of their sexual problems.

Hostility to one's spouse also figures as a very common reaction to difficulties in the marital relationship. Many an extramarital affair has been started as an attempt to "get back at" one's spouse for any number of reasons, some real and some imagined. "Tit for tat" is hardly a sound basis for extramarital relations but we have many folk sayings which cover this contingency: "What's good for the goose is good for the gander."

Self-depreciation is another common factor in some extramarital forays. Where a spouse cannot measure up to what he or she thinks is the other's expectation, he or she sometimes seeks extramarital sex as a supposedly "easier" way out than forthrightly working through the problems.

A lot of men and women seem to feel the need for bolstering their ego, and use the extramarital liaison as the means to do so. This sort of thing happens frequently in the middle years when men and women may feel their sexual attractiveness slipping away. It is somewhat reassuring to find out that one is still attractive to the other sex. There are better ways of facing one's feelings of inadequacy, however.

Escapism in general probably accounts for a considerable amount of extramarital sex relations and particularly escape from boring, dull marriages. One wife reported that she could predict exactly when her husband would ask her for sex: each night when they were walking upstairs to go to bed, when his foot hit the seventh step! Obviously this wife was ripe for an extramarital affair to escape this boring situation. Hopefully, this husband could be helped to be somewhat more spontaneous in his approaches, which might help.

A variety of sexual disturbances can contribute to extramarital affairs. Some sexual partners are impotent or frigid with their spouses but not with their extramarital partners. Some clients of mine have had sexual fixations or particular hang-ups about some specific sexual behavior which they were unable to persuade their marital partners to go along with; hence they sought outside partners to satisfy their particular sexual proclivities. It would have been better, in some sense, to get rid of the disturbance, but some clients part with their sexual disturbances very reluctantly; in fact, it is very popular these days to say that one is entitled to sex in whatever way one desires. (Ard, *Rational Sex Ethics*, 1989) This seems to deny that there is any such thing as a sexual disturbance in fact. We shall delve into this aspect more deeply in the next chapter where we shall discuss problematic sexual behavior.

So we see that there are, indeed, healthy and disturbed reasons for extramarital sexual relations. Sometimes these get mixed up, and perhaps in many instances the motivation is a mixture of both healthy and disturbed reasons. Many people assume that their reasons are always healthy ones when, in fact, they may be kidding themselves and actually have very disturbed motivations behind their actions. But, of course, in our culture, traditional or conventional values presuppose that there are *never* any healthy reasons which justify *any* extramarital sexual relations. Once again, the truth would seem to reside somewhere in between.

Perhaps the monogamous ideals which are the essence of the traditional or conventional values in our culture actually work against marriage. (Ard, 1972) In the average or conventional person's mind, it probably sounds like a contradiction in terms to even ask if monogamy (or the monogamous ideal) is destructive of marriage, since to the conventional person, marriage and monogamy are synonymous. But as anyone who has studied marriage and sexual customs in the various cultures knows, marriage and monogamy are *not* equivalent.

By way of brief review, let us define some of the relevant terms here. *Polygamy* means having a plurality of wives or husbands at the same time. *Polygyny* is where the male is allowed to have several wives. *Polyandry* is where a woman is permitted to have several husbands at the same time.

I would like to offer for your serious consideration the thesis that the *monogamous ideal,* as it is conventionally understood in our culture, *is detrimental to marriage.* (Ard, 1972) Let us be clear about just what is mean here. The monogamous ideal, as it is usually understood in conventional terms, means that *every* individual man and woman is expected to fall in love with, and marry *for life* (and in religious terms, *forever,* including life after death), *only one* member of the other sex, *and to desire no other* from that moment on.

The monogamous ideal insists that love is forever and that the "real thing" (this is, "true love") only comes *once* in a lifetime. There are severe penalties for those who do not follow this monogamous ideal. Some even think this ideal to be a part of God's plan and any variance from it, a sin against God.

Now obviously such ideas would have been relegated to the garbage can as unrealistic, unworkable, impractical and not in accord with the facts of human nature if they had not been put in religious terms and therefore out of reach of any sound, sensible discussion, debate, and resolution by scientific evidence. But, unfortunately, when a religious leader gets into this area, most people obsequiously defer to him and retire from any sane

190

discussion. Jesus is reported to have said the following: "You have heard that it was said, 'You shall not commit adultery.' But I say to you that every one who looks at a woman lustfully has already committed adultery with her in his heart." (Matthew 5, 27) And Jesus is also reported to have said, a little further on in Matthew (19, 9): "And I say to you: whoever divorces his wife, except for unchastity, and marries another, commits adultery."

As a psychologist and marriage counselor, I suggest to you that it would be hard to conceive of any laws or ideals more detrimental to the possibility of happy marriages among a people than this monogamous ideal. I am going to suggest that this monogamous ideal represents sick, twisted thinking. And yet millions of people in our culture subscribe to this sort of irrational thinking without ever questioning the underlying assumptions or looking carefully at the consequences of such beliefs. These people feel guilty and sinful if they do not measure up to this perfectionistic, self-defeating, mentally harmful nonsense.

I see husbands who feel that they are "dirty dogs" merely because they did not go blind when they got married and, afterward, upon seeing an attractive female stranger, quite understandably thought about having sexual intercourse with her. And I see in my marriage counseling practice many, many people who feel guilty and failures, simply because they are *considering* getting a divorce! In both instances, I think any fair, clear thinking done on these matters would lead to the conclusion that the conventional views on these topics embody sick, twisted thinking. (Ard, 1983, 1989) If anyone else but Jesus had said these sorts of things they would have been abandoned and forgotten long ago. But because Jesus is reported to have said them, we have had reams of paper expended on efforts to say what he "really meant," to reinterpret him, to "explain" him, to make his teachings fit in with later, more scientific, rational thinking about divorce or even admiring beautiful women after a man is married.

In anthropology, two schools of thought have been actively in conflict with each other for a number of years on the crucial issue here. One contends that the original nature of man was polygamous and the other, that it was more or less monogamous. (Calverton, 1931b, p. 478) As a result of this latter school of thought, an entirely erroneous idea of the sexual nature of the human species has been foisted upon the social sciences. These anthropologists of the "monogamous" school of thought not content, for instance, with tracing the development of marriage through its various forms, but were equally concerned with "proving" that monogamy was the ultimate state in marital evolution. (Calverton, 1931a, p. 5)

These anthropologists of the "monogamous" school of thought declared monogamy was the basic form of marriage of the human species. (Calverton, 1931a, p. 7) "Anthropology was thus made to serve as an excellent prop for the support of middle-class ethics. It defended the *status quo* by giving so-called final scientific sanction to its essential doctrines." (Calverton, 1931a, p. 8) One famous anthropologist, Westermarck, stated that "The laws of monogamy can never be changed but must be followed much more strictly than they are now." (Calverton, 1931a, p. 10)

What are the actual facts with regard to the question: Is man monogamous by nature? Obviously American society formally recognizes only one form of sexual partnership, namely monogamy. (Ford and Beach, 1951, p. 107) In cross-cultural perspective this formal attitude toward sexual relationship is exceedingly rare. (Ford and Beach, 1951, p. 107) In the most extensive cross-cultural survey made to date (Ford and Beach, 1951, pp. 107-108), where 185 different cultures were studied, the evidence reveals that formal restriction to single mateships characterizes only 29 of the cultures, or less than 16 percent. Furthermore, of these 29 societies, less than one third wholly disapprove of both premarital and extramarital liaisons.

It might be fairly accurate to conclude, without fear of contradiction, that *man is not monogamous by nature.* In fact, if we confine ourselves to the recent, serious scientists on the subject, no one has ever dared to argue that man is genuinely monogamous by nature. (Calverton, 1931b, p. 480) However, some people have reluctantly accepted the fact that men are polygamous but still insist that at least women are monogamous. But I would like to suggest that women are by nature no more monogamous than men, and no less polygamous. (Calverton, 1931b, pp. 480ff.)

The best evidence of this is to be found in those cultures where the conditions of life do not hamper the sex expression of women any more than of men. Whenever conditions have allowed it, woman has rejected the monogamous relationship as frequently as man. Granted equal freedom, woman tends to be equally variational and multiple in her sex expression. (Calverton, 1981b, p. 481) These are the facts, then, which practically every competently educated psychologist has known, but has been unwilling to declare.

Where the element of romance is most stressed (as in America), there monogamy tends to be the greater failure. (Calverton, 1931b, p. 487) It would seem a fair conclusion, then, to say that monogamy, particularly the romantic, monogamous ideal as conceived in America, is destructive of many happy, realistic, healthy marriages.

Unofficially and extralegally, America actually might be said to be a polygamous country today. That is, about one in three married couples become divorced or legally separated, and many of these divorced or separated individuals had carried on extramarital affairs for years before they actually dissolved their marriage bonds. Among those who do not legally break up their marriages, about a quarter of the women and half of the men admit to having extramarital relations at some time during their lives. (Ellis, 1962)

The monogamous ideal puts unrealistic demands and expectations into people' minds which frequently work to their detriment insofar as achieving a satisfactory adjustment in marriage is concerned. A more realistic and rational view of human nature would allow for a variety of patterns of relationships between the sexes, rather than saying that there is one legitimate sort, that is, the lifelong monogamous one. (Ard, *Rational Sex Ethics*, 1989)

From the standpoint of freedom and democracy, the polygamous societies are more open-minded and uncoercive; whereas the monogamous societies, including our own, tend to be more dogmatic, authoritarian, and restrictive. (Ellis, 1962, p. 22) If we can get people to question the monogamous ideal and eliminate it as the *only* way to govern lives as far as sexual relationships are concerned, we would provide more people with the opportunity to work out a more satisfactory sexual adjustment with as many, or as few, people of the other sex as they realistically could.

Such a freer, pluralistic view would have several advantages over the monogamous ideal. For example, it would allow for those people who have what might be called varietist's needs. If these people can arrange for multiple partners, why should they be denied? Such a freer view would also provide for the sex needs of surplus males and females. It would also permit maximum sex satisfaction; each person would seek his or her own level of satisfaction. It would minimize jealousy and possessiveness. Sex, under this pluralistic system, would entail free choice instead of forced choice. Love could be freely given instead of restrictively and jealously minimized. Human beings could become choosers of their own sex destiny rather than pieces of sexual property.

The basic statement here being made is that a more *pluralistic* arrangement could be freely *permitted* but not necessarily forced upon each individual. Let us *allow* true sexual freedom to those people who want it and can use it rationally and ethically. Let us *not force* polygamy *or monogamy* on anyone, through laws, public opinion, or the ideals we profess. The sanest society is the one which forces no one marital arrangement on anyone, while permitting all possible designs for mating for everyone. (Ellis, 1962, p. 23) The basic argument here, then is for *marital democracy,* with each individual being able to determine what sort of marital or nonmarital arrangement he or she wants to have.

There is some evidence that such a suggestion may not be entirely out of the range of possibility. Gerhard Neubeck's book on *Extra-marital Relations* (1969) offers some such evidence, as does Herbert Otto's *The New Sexuality* (1971). If a new sexuality is developing, as Otto and others have documented, perhaps this present discussion can provide some guidelines as to how to help make the new sexuality more sane, more rational, and less self-defeating for those who wish to partake of it. But if this is to be, we had better seek the answers to some of the questions Neubeck has raised:

>"Can we learn to understand that it is possible to love more than one person, to be loved by more than one person? Can we accept that? What it will mean is a reshaping of the total culture so that even the young child in the beginning of the socialization and conditioning process can learn this idea of non-exclusive love."

(Neubeck, 1969, p. 198)

And finally,

>"Are we then headed for a society in which extra-marital relationships will not occur in a clandestine fashion, but where married couples will make conscious choices, to be or not be monogamous?" (Neubeck, 1969, p. 198)

SUGGESTED FURTHER READING

Ard, Ben N., Jr. "Sexuality as a Personal and Social Force," *in* Otto, Herbert A. (Editor) *The New Sexuality* (Palo Alto: Science & Behavior Books, 1971), pp. 14-25.

Ard, Ben N., Jr. "Monogamy: Is It Destructive of Marriage? (Some Unconventional Thoughts on a Conventional Topic)," *The Marriage and Family Counselors Quarterly,* 7 (1972), 1-8.

Ard, Ben N., Jr. *Living Without Guilt and/or Blame: Conscience, Superego and Psychotherapy* (Smithtown, N.Y.: Exposition Press, 1983)

Ard, Ben Neal, Jr. *Rational Sex Ethics* (New York: Peter Lang, 2nd ed., 1989).

Calverton, V. F. "Modern Anthropology and the Theory of Cultural Compulsives," *in* Calverton, V. F. (Editor) *The Making of Man: An Outline of Anthropology* (New York: Modern Library, 1931a), pp. 1-37.

Dearborn, Lester W. "Extramarital Relations," *in* Fishbein, Morris and Burgess, Ernest W. (Editors) *Successful Marriage* (Garden City, N.Y.: Doubleday, rev. ed., 1963), pp. 157-167.

Ellis, Albert. "Adultery: Pros and Cons," *in* Ellis, Albert *Sex Without Guilt* (New York: Lyle Stuart, 1958), pp. 51-65.

Ellis, Albert. "A Plea for Polygamy," *Eros,* 1 (1962), 22-23.

Ellis, Albert. "Healthy and Disturbed Reasons for Having Extramarital Relations," *in* Neubeck, Gerhard (Editor) *Extra-marital Relations* (Englewood Cliffs, N.J.: Prentice-Hall, 1969), pp. 153-161.

Ford, Clellan S. and Beach, Frank A. *Patterns of Sexual Behavior* (New York: Harper, 1951).

Harper, Robert A. "Extramarital Relations," *in* Ellis, Albert and Abarbanel, Albert (Editors) *The Encyclopedia of Sexual Behavior* (New York: Hawthorn Books, 1961), Vol. 1, pp. 384-391.

Neubeck, Gerhard (Editor) *Extra-marital Relations* (Englewood Cliffs, N.J.: Prentice-Hall, 1969).

Otto, Herbert A. (Editor) *The New Sexuality* (Palo Alto: Science and Behavior Books, 1971).

Roy, Rustum and Roy, Della. "Is Monogamy Outdated?" *in* Kirdendall, Lester A. and Whitehurst, Robert N. (Editors) *The New Sexual Revolution* (New York: Donald W. Brown, 1971), pp. 131-148.

Taylor, Richard. *Having Love Affairs.* Buffalo: Prometheus Books, 1982.

Vannoy, Russell. *Sex Without Love: A Philosophical Exploration.* Buffalo: Prometheus Books, 1980.

"I would tend to recommend, therefore, that we stop speaking about sex deviations at all, that we drop the nasty, pejorative connotations that almost invariably go with the use of such terms, and that instead we merely try to distinguish between sexual (and nonsexual) behavior that occurs in an emotionally disturbed manner."

Albert Ellis (1976, pp. 285-286)

CHAPTER 13

PROBLEMATIC SEXUAL BEHAVIOR:
THE EROTIC MINORITIES

Not too many years ago, the material covered in this chapter would have been said to concern "sexual perversions," a term which has fallen out of favor in the field of sexology. Even "sexual deviance," which somewhat replaced the older term of perversion, still has connotations which some people think are unfortunate, to say the least.

I constantly get the perennial question from my clients, "Is such and such behavior <u>normal</u> or <u>abnormal</u>?" The whole area of sexual perversion, sexual deviance, paraphilias and so forth, including the basic questions about what is "abnormal" in the sexual areas deserves more discussion. (Wilson, 1987; Morgenthaler, 1988; Lester, 1975)

Paraphilias is another term used for those patterns which appear to many people as "different," or sometimes "weird," or "kinky," if not bizarre. (Money, 1988) Sexology as a science over the years has changed its views of just what sorts of sexual behavior can be considered abnormal. Nearly all of the aforementioned terms have connotations which imply to some people "moral" implications. Rather than introduce any such "moralistic" connotations, I prefer to refer to all such sexual behavior as <u>problematic</u> sexual behavior. People who have these sorts of sexual problems are, indeed, the erotic minorities. (Ullerstam, 1966)

Lars Ullerstam, a Swedish psychiatrist with an interest in philosophy, has written a book entitled *The Erotic Minorities* (1966) in which he argues for a more humane attitude toward the sexually deviant. When this book first appeared in the 1960's he could say that the sexual deviates were too embarrassed and too guilt ridden to dare to challenge public opinion. (1966, p. 161) But since that time, the gay liberation movement and the various organizations of other erotic minorities have become most militant and the "mirror-image" concept of counseling erotic minorities has arisen.

The mirror-image concept of counseling seems to imply that peer counseling is best for any erotic minority. That is, whether it is a matter of color, drugs, or sexual matters, the counselor best qualified to help any erotic minority (or any minority of any sort) should be someone who has had a similar if not identical background. At least the point of view of the therapist should be sympathetic with the client and work within the client's values and/or preferences. The counselor or therapist (from this mirror-image point of view) should always work to help the client achieve whatever the client wants. The basic flow in this mirror-image view of counseling or therapy will be obvious as we discuss some of the many kinds of paraphilias or problematic sexual behaviors of the various erotic minorities.

There are many kinds of problematic sexual behavior, including, for example, exhibitionism, voyeurism (i.e., "peeping Toms"), fetishism (using, for example, varies items such as shoes, panties, etc, in order to have orgasms), nymphomania, satyriasis, transvestism (cross-dressing), bestiality (using animals for sexual purposes), transsexualism (seeking changes of sex and gender through surgery and hormones), S & M (sadism and masochism, involving leathers, beatings, whippings, etc.), sexual molestation (involving forcing one's sexual attentions on unwilling partners who do not give their informed consent), rape, pedophilia (or use of children for sexual purposes), and necrophilia (use of corpses for sexual purposes), etc, etc. These are just a few of the sorts of problematic sexual behaviors which have caused problems to those who indulge in these patterns of sexual behavior. There are, of course, some people who have indulged in these sorts of behaviors but deny that they have ever had any difficulty except for what they would term society's oppression of them for being "different."

I have dealt with these sorts of problematic sexual behavior on the part of clients over the years and have come to the conclusion that many people are "shocked" and very upset by these sorts of behavior. I have been training graduate students to become counselors for many years and have come to the conclusion that the professional person working in these areas had better become what I have termed "shockproof" or "unflappable" and convey to his or her clients, whatever their problem, the point of view expressed by the ancient Roman, Marcus Aurelius: "Nothing human is foreign to me." Clients can thus come to believe that the professional person helping them will not react with horror or moral indignation at whatever sort of problematic sexual behavior that is being discussed. And even if the professional person is not a "mirror-image" of the client and may not have had the particular experience the client is discussing, the professional therapist can be of assistance to the client.

Although those in the helping professions need not (and had better not) make moralistic judgments about problematic sexual behaviors (because it is counterproductive to the client for the professional therapist to do so), this definitely does not mean that the professional should make no value judgments at all, as some have contended. Professional therapists had better inquire persistently as to what the consequences have been and may probably be in the future for a given client, and whether or not his or her behavior contributes to or detracts from his or her happiness in the long run (not merely the short run). This explains why we as professionally trained sex therapists and psychotherapists had better not say that the drug addict (or junkie), or the client with a compulsive sexual hang-up, is "happy" (that is, *really* happy), even if the drug addict could always get all he or she wanted of his or her favorite drug, or the compulsive person could practice his or her compulsion as often as desired. We, as professionals, cannot content ourselves with merely recording and reflecting how the subject appraised his or her life *from his or her point of view;* we ourselves had better learn to make a scientific, professional appraisal, not merely report on somebody else's appraisal (that is, the client's or the layperson's point of view).

The client's point of view can be distorted; in fact, it is just in the sorts of cases discussed in this area of life that the clients frequently are distorted in their views of their sexual behaviors and the probable consequences. Not that they always are, it goes without saying. The fact that the client says he or she "likes" what he or she is doing, and desires to continue, had better not be the final say on the matter. The consequences had better be considered (and long-term consequences, not merely short-term). And by someone professionally trained to know the wide range of possibilities from a scientific point of view.

For example, many transvestites may essentially want to be left alone to pursue their compulsions about cross-dressing. Although they may also wish that society could be educated toward a more tolerant attitude toward cross-dressing. If such transvestites live a "normal" or "usual" sex life (some such men being married and have usual sex relations with their wives) they may not harm anyone, particularly if their wives are very understanding.

Transvestites (or cross-dressers) come with all sorts of sexual patterns, however, Some cross-dressers just dress up in women's clothes in the privacy of their own homes. They otherwise live a "normal" sex life with their wives. Some such wives are able to tolerate such cross-dressing.

Other men have started cross-dressing later moved over into transsexualism where they want to use hormones and surgery to change themselves into a woman. Modern surgery can do amazing things, such as removing a man's penis and testicles, and constructing a "vagina" but the bottom line is that after the best of such surgery it is not possible for this newly created "woman" to ever have a baby. So what we have is thus only a castrated and mutilated man who can never function completely as a male or a female.

Harry Benjamin, one of the early leaders in dealing with transsexual and transvestite phenomena, has said that

> "There are instances, however, when transvestism may be a great handicap for the patient and he would then be ready to undergo treatment with the hope of being cured of his strange and embarrassing compulsion." (Harry Benjamin, *The Transsexual Phenomenon*, 1966, pp. 110-111)

Psychotherapy would then be the method of choice (rather than surgery), and as Harry Benjamin says, "If the patient persists long enough in an honest wish to be cured ("honest" at least in his conscious mind), success may be attained. (Benjamin, 1966, p. 111) The form of psychotherapy applied in such cases, as Benjamin notes, depends entirely on the attitude of the therapist. (1966, p. 111) Benjamin adds an additional note: "Part of the creative treatment would have to be removal from transvestitic temptations, friends, transvestitic literature, and the like, as completely as possible." (1966, p. 111)

Deborah Heller Feinbloom, who has written a book on *Transvestites & Transsexuals* (1976), has concluded that

> *"It seems to me that by their theories Money and Ehrhart have demonstrated that the <u>learned</u> nature of gender dimorphism (these authors conclude that <u>learning</u> seems to be the main source of gender dimorphism, despite their exhaustive survey of physiological factors)."* (Feinbloom, 1976, p. 281) (Emphasis added.)

Feinbloom has estimated that there are probably about 10,000 transsexuals in the U.S., 2,000 of whom have had surgery. (1976, p. 25) And this despite the scientific fact that transsexuals rarely have chromosomal or hormonal abnormalities. (Feinbloom, 1976, p. 25)

The English psychiatrist, Clifford Allen, in his book *Textbook of Psycho-sexual Disorders* (1969), when discussing transsexualism, has said

> *"Obviously mutilating surgery is not the solution for such patients. The aim should be not to make the <u>normal</u> body fit the <u>abnormal</u> psyche but vice versa."* (Allen, 1969, pp 296-297) (Emphasis in the original.)

Dr. Allen says, "If the patient can be persuaded to accept psychotherapy this is the treatment of choice,. . ." (Allen, 1969, p. 297)

Turning to another problematic sexual behavior, one that shocks many in our urban society, let's consider bestiality. Bestiality, or having sexual relations with animals, is one form of problematic sexual behavior that appears particularly offensive, obnoxious, or shocking to many lay people. Yet bestiality has been reported in almost all societies in some form or other. How are we to understand such behavior? In our culture, boys who have been reared to think that sex before marriage is sinful, bad, evil and wrong, and who have contact with farm animals (sheep, mules, chickens, dogs, cows, horses, and so forth) have been known to use a variety of animals for sexual purposes.

On one of the islands of the Caribbean some young boys were reported to have committed sodomy with chickens. This island culture was more advanced than our own in some respects in that the informants from this culture felt that the bestiality in these cases was a substitute for normal sexual relations and thus did not present any cause for alarm.

The practice of bestiality is not limited to males, of course. Girls have used animals for sexual purposes, also. For example, girls have been reported to use dogs for cunnilingus. Once again, the majority of the society where a girl was reported to have used dogs in this fashion did not think such behavior warranted collective negative sanctions because, as they reported, the girls were living in an isolated area at the time the practice began, where no male sexual partners were available. A very understanding culture, compared to ours.

Where isolation from the more usual sexual outlets provides a situation where some humans resort to bestiality (for example, a sheepherder using sheep sexually on an isolated mountaintop), the question comes down to what does the person do when he comes down from the mountaintop? If he continues to seek out sheep when women are readily available, I would say he has a problem, whether he thinks so or not. The setting up of sexual habit patterns are understandable from a psychological point of view, but that is not to say that they _have_ to be continued compulsively, particularly if they are self-defeating in the long run.

Since the revolt against psychiatry has arisen in recent years, there have arisen "special interest groups" made up of people who have various problematic sexual behavior problems but who do not want to turn to any of the helping professions for assistance unless they know that the member of the helping professions is "one of them" or at least sympathetic to their point of view. There are newsletters published by and for transvestites, transsexuals, etc. And these days some clients come in for therapy but they do not want their therapist to question or confront their life style. Some professionals in the field go along with such clients and accept whatever sexual pattern the clients have adopted. And yet, as the English psychiatrist Clifford Allen has said, "It is unwise to accept the theorizing of sufferers as valid because of the intense need to rationalize their behavior." (1969, p. 296) And to _rationalize_ one's behavior is _not_ to be _rational_ about it.

The form of psychotherapy that seems most helpful to people with various sexual problems of the sort we have been discussing in this book would seem to be psychotherapy of a very philosophical sort, psychotherapy that gets down to the philosophical basics about one's assumptions, ideas and life decisions. Such a psychotherapy is exemplified by Rational-Emotive Therapy. A cognitive form of psychotherapy seems indicated since most of the resulting problems are not usually in the genitals but rather in the mind.

For those who might like to know if there is a rational-emotive therapist near where they live, they must inquire at the Institute for

Rational-emotive Therapy, 45 East 65th Street, New York, N.Y. 10021. (212) 535-0822.

John Money (1988) has described how an antiandrogen (Depo-Provera) may be used, in connection with counseling, for the treatment of paraphilia sex offenders. In describing Depo-Provera, John Money has said

"It suppresses or lessens the frequency of erection and ejaculation and also lessens the feeling of the sexual drive and the mental imagery of sexual arousal. To illustrate: for the pedophile there will be a decreased erotic attraction to children. This medication can be thought of as a suppressant of the feeling of sex drive, intended to make self-governance easier, usually with the help of individual or couple counseling as well." (Money, 1988, p. 232)

Paraphilia is really a love disorder, not a sex disorder, according to John Money (1988) and Fritz Moregenthaler (1988). The aim of the counseling or therapy sessions in working with the paraphilias, as stated by Money is given as follows:

"These sessions are intended to help the patient establish a new life style and to cope with problems that have developed as a consequence of his or her prior life style. Therapy may be either individual or in a group." (Money, 1988, p. 236)

SUGGESTED FURTHER READING

Allen, Clifford, "Perversion, Sexual," *in* Ellis, Albert and Abarbanel, Albert
(Editors), *The Encyclopedia of Sexual Behavior* (New York:
Hawthorn Books, 1961), vol 2, pp. 802-811.

Allen, Clifford. *A Textbook of Psychosexual Disorders* (London: Oxford
University Press, 2nd ed., 1969).

Ard, Ben N., Jr. "The Case of the Black and Silver Masochist," *in* Ellis,
Albert, et al, *Growth Through Reason: Verbatim Cases in Rational-
Emotive Therapy* (Palo Alto: Science & Behavior Books, 1971), pp.
15-45.

Benjamin, Harry. *The Transsexual Phenomenon* (New York: Warner Books,
1966.)

Ellis, Albert. "Sexual Deviations," *in* Ellis, Albert, *The Art and Science of
Love* (New York: Lyle Stuart, 1960), pp. 248-303.

Ellis, Albert. *Sex and the Liberated Man* (Syracuse, N.J.: Lyle Stuart,
1976).

Feinbloom, Deborah Heller. *Transvestites & Transsexuals: Mixed Views*
(New York: Delta Book, 1976)

214

Gagnon, John H. and Simon, William (Editors) *Sexual Deviance* (New York: Harper & Row, 1967).

Lester, David. *Unusual Sexual Behavior: The Standard Deviations* (Springfield, Illinois: Charles Thomas, 1975).

Money, John. *Gay, Straight, and In-Between: The Sexology of Erotic Orientation* (New York: Oxford university Press, 1988).

Morgenthaler, Fritz. *Homosexuality, Heterosexuality, Perversion* (Hillsdale, N.J.: Atlantic Press. 1988).

Ostow, Mortimer (Editor) *Sexual Deviation: Psychoanalytic Insights* (New York: Quadrangle, 1974).

Outreach Beacon. The Outreach Beacon is the official publication of the Human Outreach and Achievement Institute. It is published four times a year and subscriptions are $15.00 per annum. All inquiries to the Outreach Beacon should be addressed to the Outreach Institute, Box 368, Kenmore Station, Boston, MA 02215. The Beacon serves as a resource for helping professionals transsexuals, cross-dressers and androgens.

Raymond, Janice G. *The Transsexual Empire* (Boston: Beacon Press, 1979).

Ullerstam, Lars. *The Erotic Minorities* (New York: Grove Press, 1966).

Wilson, Glenn D. (Editor)   *Variant Sexuality: Research and Theory* (London: Groom Helm, 1987).

"Sexual sanity (like nonsexual sanity), then, largely consists of noncompulsiveness, of personal experimentation, of open mindedness, of sticking to pathways that do not entail too many practical disadvantages, and perhaps above all, of accepting yourself and utterly refusing to down yourself even if you do the wrong thing and indubitably behave self-defeatingly."

Albert Ellis (*Sex and the Liberated Man*, 1976, p. 300)

CHAPTER 14

HOMOSEXUALS, LESBIANS, AND
THE GAY LIBERATION MOVEMENT

The views on homosexuality and lesbianism have been in state of flux, to say the least, in recent years, from the 1950's through the 1960's. (D'Emilio & Freedman, 1988) One can find in the literature (both professional and lay) a wide variety of stances taken on homosexuality and lesbianism, from the most extreme homophobic, condemning, moralistic judgments, usually from religious fanatics on the "right" (fundamentalists), all the way to extremely homophile ("liberal") statements made by people trying to "justify" just about any and all behavior of homosexuals and lesbians, and attempts to deny any critical statements made by anyone about homosexuality (which seems to imply that homosexuals are not responsible or accountable for any of their sexual behavior).

Obviously, since I have been a practicing psychotherapist during these changing times (from the 1960's through the 1980's) and have had clients with homosexual problems of various kinds, I have always thought that neither the homophobic nor the homophile stances were appropriate for anyone attempting to provide scientific psychotherapy of a deeply philosophical sort. So I shall present scientific facts (both pro and con on various issues) and hope the reader will not assume that the position of this writer is either homophobic nor homophilic, but rather that of a professional, scientific scholar.

C. A. Tripp has written a very sympathetic book about *The*

220

Homosexual Matrix (1987) in which he says:

> *"That homosexuality raises the level of neurosis in many of its participants, and that it seriously disturbs a few others, are facts which, though localized, do ultimately amount to social liabilities."*

(Tripp, 1987, p. 258)

Masters and Johnson, in their book on *Homosexuality in Perspective* (1979), have said

> *"When dealing with problems of sexual preference, it is vital that all health-care professionals bear in mind that the homosexual man or woman is basically a man or woman by genetic determination and is homosexually oriented by <u>learned</u> preference."*
>
> *(Masters & Johnson, 1979, p. 271 [Emphasis added.]*

The esteemed historian of psychotherapy, Robert A. Harper, in an article on "Psychological Aspects of Homosexuality," has said

> *"One peculiarity in the antisexuality that surrounds the homosexual in his childhood home is that the controlling parent, often the parent of the other sex than the child's, has his puritanical attitudes sharply focused on heterosexuality. This parent often closes, locks, and seals the door to heterosexual expression and orientation for the child, but leaves the door to homosexuality relatively unguarded and possibly even open a little."*

(Robert A. Harper, in Beigel, *Advances in Sex Research,* 1963, p. 189)

THE GAY LIBERATION MOVEMENT

The politicalization of the diagnosis of homosexuality by the psychiatric profession has been documented in a book by Ronald Bayer, *Homosexuality and American Psychiatry* (1987). In 1973, homosexuality was removed from the official list of mental diseases (the <u>Diagnostic and Statistical Manual of Psychiatric Disorders</u>). The leadership of the American Psychiatric Association was charged by some with "an unseemly capitulation to the threats and pressures of Gay Liberation groups." (Bayer, 1987, p. 3)

As Bayer stated in his introduction to his well documented book,

> *"The entire process, from the first confrontations by gay demonstrators at psychiatric conventions to the referendum demanded by orthodox psychiatrists, seemed to violate the most basic expectations about how questions of science should be resolved."* (Bayer, 1987, p. 3)

The militant Gay liberation groups challenged every instance of authority in scientific forums and "compelled psychiatric experts to negotiate the pathological status of homosexuality with homosexuals themselves." (Bayer, 1987, p. 3)

> *"The result was not a conclusion based on an approximation of the scientific truth as dictated by reason, but was instead an action demanded by the ideological temper of the times."* (Bayer, 1987, pp. 3-4)

By the late 1960's the thrusts of the early leaders of the Gay liberation movement had become what Bayer has termed "a full-blown attack, with homosexuality presented as an 'alternative life style' worthy of social acceptance on a par with heterosexuality." (Bayer, 1987, p. 8)

"Like so many other client populations, homosexuals turned on those formerly perceived as protectors, their sense of self-confidence enhanced by an awareness that they were part of an upsurge of protest directed at every social institution in America. Thus American psychiatry emerged as a primary target of their radical disenchantment." (Bayer, 1987, p. 8)

Even the gay newspaper *The Advocate* has commented on the disruptive gay militants:

". . .it becomes more and more apparent that the so-called gay militants are not so much pro-gay as they are anti-establishment, anti-capitalist, anti-society. They lash out in all directions, destroying everything in sight - gay or straight." (Quoted in Bayer, 1987, p. 96)

A final conclusion from the Bayer book:

"That the American Psychiatric Association responded to the concerted pressure of an angry, militant movement that had made full use of coercive and intimidating tactics is undeniable." (Bayer, 1987, p. 189)

HYPOTHESES ABOUT HOMOSEXUALITY

John Money, a psychologist at Johns Hopkins Medical School, has developed a concept of "lovemaps" ("a personalized, developmental representation or template in the mind and in the brain that depicts the idealized lover and the idealized program of sexuoerotic activity with that lover"). (Money, 1988, p. 127) This "lovemaps" concept or hypothesis can be applied to heterosexuals, homosexuals and paraphiliacs.

And John Money, who has written several books sympathetic to homosexuals, has made this criticism of the gay liberation movement:

> *"The gay movement, because of its focus on the struggle for gay political rights, has not properly differentiated gay rights from paraphiliac rights; nor has it recognized the potential hazards of the more dangerous paraphiliac either to gay individuals or to the political reputation of the movement."* (Money, 1988, p. 181)

And Money has made an even more devastating criticism of the gay activists:

> *"For the same reasons that some gay activists repudiate the medical model, they repudiate also biomedical research into the developmental origins of homosexuality and, as a consequence, into the origins of heterosexuality and bisexuality also. They are no less vociferous in repudiating social research, especially if it is designed to seek causes of homosexuality as psychogenic deviancy from the heterosexual norm."* (Money, 1988, p. 153)

It would not seem unfair to point out that the gay liberation movement, growing up as it did during the counter-culture (hippie) movement, is fundamentally anti-science and anti-intellectual, a "know-nothing" sort of movement. And this is most sad since science is the only place the gays can turn for assistance for their most terrible epidemic, that of AIDS. AIDS is killing thousands of people, both homosexual and heterosexual because there is no medical cure available at the present time.

And the gay liberation rejection of scientific therapists blocks gays off from getting the psychotherapeutic help which could help them change some of their sexual behavior patterns. The advent of an epidemic of AIDS may have very lethal consequences for the homosexual community if homosexuals refuse to give up certain patterns of oral and anal sex practices (e.g., fellatio, fisting, rimming), particularly with anonymous, promiscuous sex partners (at "tea rooms" and "glory holes"). As John Money has said, "The consequences of sexual anonymity in the new era of AIDS may be lethal." (Money, 1988, p. 154)

Commenting on the aims of psychotherapy with homosexuals, Albert Ellis has said,

> "In the course of psychotherapy, the homosexual individual may also be helped to accept his homosexuality without the enormous amounts of guilt and anxiety that usually accompany inversion. But if an exclusive homosexual is only enabled, through psychotherapy, to accept homosexuality, and if he is not in any way released from the neurotic fixations, phobias, obsessions, and/or compulsions which are forcing him to be exclusively homosexual, then very little real therapy has been accomplished, and he is still as basically neurotic as when he first came in for treatment. . . . When people tell me that homosexuals are incurable and I think of the twenty years I have been curing them, . . .I answer 'They're not.' And have done with it." (Albert Ellis, quoted in Daniel Wiener, 1988, pp. 101-102)

The above quote touches not only on what kind of psychotherapy homosexuals may obtain from some psychotherapists but also touches on what may be termed the "incurable hypothesis."

THE INCURABLE HYPOTHESIS

The homophile writers and the gay movement in general do not like to think that any homosexual can ever be "cured." The Gay liberation movement will not tolerate a different point of view than their own. They ignore any professional person who differs with their point of view. In books written by homophiles, they frequently just leave out any reference to professionals who have written about curing homosexuals, such as Clifford Allen, Berg, Bieber, Albert Ellis, Robert A. Harper, Hatterer, Socarides, etc., etc. But don't take my word for this hypothesis of mine; check it out by checking the index of authors cited in any such book about gays. If you do not find any reference to any of the above authors who have offered evidence regarding cures, then you know the book is by an homophile who does not want to cite any evidence for a view contrary to that of the gay community. As Socarides has pointed out in discussing recent developments regarding homosexuality and the gay liberation groups,

". . .militant homosexual groups continued to attack any psychiatrist or psychoanalyst who dared to present his findings as to the psychopathology of homosexuality before national or local meetings of psychiatrists or in public forums." (Socarides, 1975, p. 87)

The incurable hypothesis, or the untreatable hypothesis has been spoken to by Albert Ellis, as follows:

"An unusually large number of writers who have stoutly held that homosexuality is incurable, such as L. Allen, Carpenter, Hirschfeld, Mercer, Vincent, and Wildeblood, turn out themselves to be confirmed homosexuals. This may be publicly stated because these writers are either now dead or have recently in print confessed to being homosexuals." (Albert Ellis, quoted in Beigel,

226

1963, p. 176)

In regard to the hypothesis about the physiological cause of homosexuality, Albert Ellis has stated

"I reviewed the evidence for the physiological causation of homoeroticism years ago and concluded that no clear-cut data existed to show that physical rather than psychological factors lead people into confirmed homosexual pathways." (Albert Ellis, *Sex and the Liberated Man,* 1976, p. 297)

Homophile writers have claimed that conclusions based on clinical cases do not justify anything much about other homosexuals who have never been in for any treatment in any therapist's office. About this matter, Albert Ellis has stated

"A very high percentage of confirmed homosexuals that I have talked with - and this again includes scores who have not come to see me or any other psychotherapist for help and many who do not consider themselves disturbed - have the typical symptoms, not merely of serious neurosis, but of borderline psychosis. They have what Dr. Paul Meehl calls cognitive slippage, in spite of their intelligence, and find great difficulty making some of the finer discriminations required for adequate social relations." (Albert Ellis, *Sex and the Liberated Man,* 1976, p. 295)

Robert A Harper, a psychologist of many years experience in Washington, D.C., has written about the psychological components of homosexuality as follows:

"The three main psychological components of homosexuality as they emerge in the writer's clinical practice are: (1) a basic anti-

227

sexuality or puritanism - an early instilled and well reinforced non-acceptance of sexuality in general and heterosexuality in particular; (2) low personal self-esteem and self-confidence - that is, deep-seated feelings of inadequacy, immaturity, and insecurity; and (3) compulsive adherence to the continually reinforced homosexual mode of orgastic satisfaction." (Harper, in Beigel, 1963, p. 187)

SUGGESTED FURTHER READING

Ard, Ben Neal, Jr. *Rational Sex Ethics.* New York: Peter Lang, 2nd edition, 1989.

Bayer, Ronald. *Homosexuality and American Psychiatry: The Politics of Diagnosis.* Princeton, N.J.: Princeton University Press, 1987.

Berg, Charles, & Allen, Clifford. *The Problem of Homosexuality.* New York: Citadel Press, 1958.

Cory, Donald Webster. *The Homosexual in America.* New York: Greenberg, 1951.

D'Emilio, John & Freedman, Estelle B. *Intimate Matters: A History of Sexuality in America.* New York: Harper & Row, 1988.

Diamant, Louis (Editor) *Male and Female Homosexuality: Psychological Approaches.* Washington: Hemisphere, 1987.

Ellis, Albert, "Constitutional Factors in Homosexuality: A Re-examination of the Evidence," pp. 161-186, *in* Beigel, Hugo G. (Editor) *Advances in Sex Research.* New York: Hoeber, 1963.

Ellis, Albert. *Homosexuality: Its Causes and Cure.* New York: Lyle Stuart, 1965.

230

Ellis, Albert. *Sex and the Liberated Man.* Secaucus, N.J.: Lyle Stuart, 1976.

Goldstein, Bernard. *Introduction to Human Sexuality.* New York: McGraw-Hill, 1976.

Haeberle, Erwin J. *The Sex Atlas.* New York: Seabury Press, 1978.

Harper, Robert A., "Psychological Aspects of Homosexuality," *in* Beigel, Hugo G. (Editor) *Advances in Sex Research.* New York: Hoeber, 1963, pp. 187-197.

Hatterer, Lawrence J. *Changing Homosexuality in the Male.* New York: McGraw-Hill, 1970.

Hetrick, Emery S. & Stein, Terry S. (Editors) *Innovations in Psychotherapy with Homosexuals.* Washington: American Psychiatric press, 1984.

Karlen, Arno. *Sexuality and Homosexuality: A New View.* New York: Norton, 1971.

Masters, William H. & Johnson, Virginia E. *Homosexuality In Perspective.* Boston: Little, Brown, 1979.

Money, John. *Gay, Straight, and In-Between: The Sexology of Erotic Orientation.* New York: Oxford University Press, 1988.

Socarides, Charles W. *Beyond Sexual Freedom.* New York: Quadrangle Books, 1975.

Stein, Terry S. & Cohen, Carol J. *Contemporary Perspectives on Psychotherapy with Lesbians and Gay Men.* New York: Plenum, 1986.

Tripp, C. A. *The Homosexual Matrix.* New York: New American Library, 1987.

Wiener, Daniel N. *Albert Ellis: Passionate Skeptic.* New York: Praeger, 1988.

Willis, Stanley E. *Understanding and Counseling the Male Homosexual.* Boston: Little, Brown, 1967.

Wolman, Benjamin B. & Money, John (Editors) *Handbook of Human Sexuality.* Englewood, Cliffs, N.J.: Prentice-Hall, 1980.

"Within reasonable limits sex represents one of the best ways for human beings to draw close to each other, but if it is the only or prime basis of a relationship, there is an extra-heavy demand that it be continuously successful, varied, and stimulating. It seems likely that a single area of activity cannot carry a relationship for very long. . .heterosexual relationships dependent almost entirely upon sex cannot be long maintained. The hope of long-lasting closeness based exclusively upon sex seems likely to be frustrated again and again."

Daniel N. Wiener
("Sexual Problems in Clinical Experience,"
quoted in Broderick & Bernard,
1969, p. 337)

CHAPTER 15

LOVE AND SEX:
THE VARYING CONTEXTS IN WHICH SEX CAN OCCUR

The interrelationship of love and sex causes many people all sorts of problems. I sometimes think Americans in particular have the greatest difficulties in this area, probably because of their unquestioned assumptions and unchallenged presumptions and premises about sex and love. I have hesitated to deal with the subject of love because probably more words have been misspent on this topic than any other. I certainly did not elect to contribute more senseless pages about the subject of love but, because so many of the clients I have seen over the years have had serious problems centering around the demarcation of love and sex, I concluded that the subject deserves further attention. As Abe Maslow has said, "We must understand love; we must be able to teach it, to create it, to predict it, or else the world is lost to hostility and to suspicion." (Maslow, 1970, p. 181)

The central problem in this area seems to be one of ascertaining the relationship between love and sex. Some people apparently keep the two always separate; for others, they overlap and are sometimes difficult to distinguish. The world's first woman's magazine, *Godey's Lady's Book,* defined love as follows: "An alliance of friendship and lust; if the former predominates, it is passion exalted and refined; but if the latter, gross and sensual." To show how the two get intertwined, Bernhard Bauer said, "Since there is no love without sexuality, we must now, if we are to understand love, try to secure clear ideas concerning the manifestations of sexuality."

(Bauer, *Woman and Love,* 1927, I, p. 153)

Many Americans are confused as to the relationship between love and sex. Our culture has for too long taught that love is the "higher" of the two concepts and that sex is definitely the lower. The Judeo-Christian traditional morality has maligned sex for so long that even people who are "not religious" (i.e., do not go to church) are still influenced by these traditional views of Christianity which are essentially antisex. (Ard, 1989)

Some people still assume that love can be "pure" (i.e., uncontaminated with sex), but Eduard von Hartmann has stated that "An assumed love without sensuality is merely a fleshless and bloodless phantom of the creative imagination.' (Hartmann, *Philosophy of the Unconscious,* 1974, p. 196) We even have a name for this nonsexual love; it is called "platonic."

Part of the problem regarding love and sex, for many people, is on what basis a marriage should be entered into, if one wants the marriage to last. Should the relationship be based on sex? Should one only marry "for love"? George Bernard Shaw, as usual, said it well: "People in love are under the influence of the most violent, insane, most illusive and transient of passions, and they are required to swear that they will remain in that excited, abnormal, exhausting condition until death do them part."

And yet we know - at least some surveys indicate - that only 32 percent of all grown women actually manage to marry and hold onto the men they love. That means 58 percent either go to the altar with the wrong groom or sometime thereafter lose the "right" one. (*San Francisco Chronicle,* April 8, 1972, p. 31)

Part of the problem involving love and sex in our culture arises from the traditional (but false) equation of sex with reproduction. This was followed with the unquestioned assumption that sex should therefore only occur where reproduction is at least a possibility, and consequently sex was limited, in this conventional view, to marriage. But as Havelock Ellis has clearly pointed out,

> "The functions of sex on the psychic and emotional side are of far greater extension than any act of procreation, they may even exclude it altogether, and when we are concerned with the welfare of the individual human being we must enlarge our outlook and deepen our insight." (Havelock Ellis, quoted in Wile, 1934, p. 26)

It has been said (Ard, 1969, p. 57) that women want love, and use sex to get it, while men want sex, and talk of love to get it. This may be an obvious oversimplification and an over generalization, but there would seem to be some element of truth in it. Thus we have some basis for the "battle between the sexes." Our culture has contributed to this conflict of interest between the sexes. As the other Ellis (Albert) has pointed out:

> "Many males in our culture are so thwarted by our sex codes and become so sex-hungry that they begin to see females only as sex objects and to depreciate any nonsexual attributes that they may have. In their turn, millions of our women become so resentful of the fact that men's interest in them is almost primarily sexual that they become misanthropic and after a while find it almost impossible to love any man." (Albert Ellis, If This Be Sexual Heresy, 1963, p. 208)

What men and women want from life with regard to sex and love are frequently different in our society because of the influence of culture.

"Again largely because of our different ways of raising males and females, the former are usually mainly obsessed with having premarital and adulterous affairs, while the latter are intent on confining their sex relations to monogamous marriage. This means that the sex goals of men and women are quite different in many instances, and that the men begin to resent the women for not, as they say in the vernacular, "putting out," while the women resent the men for being sexually exploitative and for not being as interested in marrying as they are." (Albert Ellis, *If This Be Sexual Heresey,* 1963, p. 208)

Some people seem to believe that sex is better in a context of love and/or affection. Others have maintained that sex can be good even without love. Russell Vannoy has written a deeply philosophical exploration of sex without love and has come out for a liberal position:

"For these reasons many liberals would eschew sex with love. Even if they happened to believe that sex with love provides more pleasure, they might want to avoid love, because to surrender one's heart to another and become dependent for one's happiness on the unpredictable emotions of another human being is hardly compatible with being a liberated, free person." (Russell Vannoy, *Sex Without Love: A Philosophical Exploration,* 1980, p. 123)

If the battle between the sexes is to be lessened in the future, with less rather than more polarization in the 1990's, we would be wise to reduce the beliefs in some of the "myths" about love (particularly "romantic" love). That prolific writer about sex, Albert Ellis, has spelled out several myths about love that are very common in our culture. (Albert Ellis, 1954, 1958)

1.   The myth that love is mysterious and that no one knows what it is. On the face of it (if one asks many different people what they think love is) there may be some evidence for this view. But love can be studied, can be handled in a rational fashion, and does not have to be completely irrational and emotional, as it often is.

2.   The myth that there is such a thing as "real" or "true" love. Some amusing evidence has shown that if there is such a thing, then it is always ahead of one in point of time, since as one looks back on the loves one may have had, they do not seem to be "true." Maybe we had better get rid of the notion of "true" or "romantic" love. (Of course, there are some authorities in the field who argue in favor of the concept of romantic love, such as Robert Blood, Nathaniel Branden and Roger Callahan, just to give a few examples.)

3.   The myth that it is difficult to tell when one is in love. Of course, if love is conceived as something mysterious, mystical and even somewhat supernatural (or otherworldly), and, as the first myth states, no one really knows what it is, then, indeed, it may prove very difficult to tell when one is in love. Then people frequently turn to tea leaves, crystal balls, psychics and other occult phenomena in the false hope of finding the right answer. But if we can simplify some of the romantic notions abut love which are so common in our culture, then people will realistically be better able to tell whether or not they are in love.

4.   The myth that love and marriage always go together. This is one of the basic "shoulds" of our conventional culture. At least it is the myth to which most of the lip service is given by the magazines, other mass media, and traditional religious teachings. But obviously one may love more

than merely one person in this life, and may, or may not, marry them all. Probably one would not even want to marry everyone with whom one might fall in love in a lifetime.

5.   The myth that one can truly love only one person at a time. This is a very basic assumption on the part of many people and one that causes considerable difficulty and consternation in many of my clients when they discover that they do, in fact, love more than one person at the same period in their life (difficult as it may be to love two people at the same instant).

One client I shall never forget caught me in a trap by asking whether I thought she would be with her dead husband in heaven one day. Since she was grieving in a heartbreaking way and seemed to want some reassurance (and I was trying to be somewhat supportive at that point), I replied: "I am sure you will." However, she played a "gotcha" on me by saying, "Well, Dr. Ard, that has puzzled me, since I was his second wife, and I wondered which one of us was going to get him in heaven." Obviously it would have been better to tell this woman that I did not know whether or not she would be with her husband in heaven (and did not know of any scientific way to even determine any way to find out), rather than hiding behind myths (mystical or supernatural) about "one and only loves" or "loves that last forever" (even into eternity).

6.   The myth that when one truly loves, one has no sex desires for individuals whom one doesn't love. This belief has troubled many a wife who has come into my office wondering why her husband, who does love her, could possibly have sexual desires for other women (who he admittedly does not love). Jesus has contributed to many people having difficulty in

this area by stating (supposedly) something to the effect that to lust after another man's wife is as bad as doing the dirty deed (obviously, not a direct quote). But Abe Maslow would seem to have pointed out a concept in this regard that exemplifies much better mental health. He has stated that, with regard to psychologically healthy people (he calls them self-actualizing people), they acknowledge sexual attraction to members of the other sex. What they *do* about it is what is important, *not* merely admitting to having the desires.

> *"For example, in spite of the fact that these people are relatively less driven to love affairs outside the marriage, yet they are much more free than the average to admit to the fact of sexual attraction to others. My impression is that there tends to be a rather easy relationship with the opposite sex, along with casual acceptance of the phenomenon of being attracted to other people, at the same time that these individuals do rather less about this attraction than other people. Also it seems to me that their talk about sex is considerably more free and casual and unconventional than the average."* (Maslow, 1970, pp. 188-189)

7. The myth that one must love one's beloved steadily or constantly all the time. One client of mine, a young woman who was a student at a midwestern university, was engaged to a young man in the service at the time. She came into my office at the university student health service and expressed doubts about whether or not her love for her fiance was real or true. When I asked why she had these doubts, she said that her love for her boyfriend was not steady and unwavering. It was strong when he was near her, when he came home on leaves; but when he

was away for long periods of time, she found she was just as happy and interested in her studies and campus life. She felt guilty about going down to the local bar where the students hung out and having fun with others, since her fiance was away in the service. She assumed that her love must be maintained at its white-hot peak all the time, else it was not "true love." More people would be better off if we helped dispose of this myth and let everyone know that love does indeed fluctuate over time and that that is quite normal.

One of the questions in this area which plague many people who are committed to the concept of "romantic" love is whether having sex without such romantic love is ever justified. (Cf. Ellis, 1958, Chapter 5) I have seen many clients who have kidded themselves that they were in love in order to justify their having sexual relations when they themselves later admitted that they were not really in love at all. That is, I have had many clients (mostly females - although some males, too) who have assumed that sex without love is somehow base, if not beneath one. (Cf. Vannoy, 1980) If we could remove some of the myths surrounding the conventional cultural concepts of romantic love, then perhaps more people could see that sex for its own sake is justified on occasion. (Cf. Loudin, *The Hoax of Romance,* 1981)

Can a man and a woman, with both eyes wide open, well aware of what they are doing (without conning each other or deluding themselves, or exploiting each other), have satisfactory (pleasant, enjoyable, ethical) sex, without being in love? I think the rational answer to that question, based upon experience with many clients (and the philosophical analysis of such people as Ellis, 1958 and Vannoy, 1980) is that sex can be an enjoyable and ethical experience, even when there is no love or any long-term commitment. Many people have reported that to me.

Maslow (1970, Chapter 12), in describing love in self-actualizing people (or psychologically health people), has reported that his subjects used the word *love* warily and with circumspection. But he also reported that sex and love can be, and most often are, more perfectly fused with each other in these psychologically healthy people. Love and sex are separable concepts and no purpose would be served in confusing them with each other unnecessarily; still, Maslow reports that they tend to become joined and merged in the loves of these self-actualizing people.

Regarding the separation of love and sex, Maslow has stated, "We cannot go so far as some who say that any person who is capable of having sexual pleasure where there is no love must be a sick man." (Maslow, 1970, p. 187) Everyone might not agree with Maslow's conclusions, but he did say that

> *"It is certainly fair to say that self-actualizing men and women tend on the whole not to seek sex for its own sake, or to be satisfied with it alone when it comes. I am not sure that my data permit me to say that they would rather not have sex at all if came without affection, but I am quite sure that I have a fair number of instances in which for the time being at least sex was given up or rejected because it came without love and affection."*
> (Maslow, 1970, p. 187)

Perhaps it would be fair to suggest here that Maslow is not talking about romantic love but rather mature love. And I would agree that sex is better in a context of love and affection, but that does not mean that sex should never be indulged in unless one is in love with one's partner. Affection between the partners always seems to add to the sexual enjoyment, but love is not always absolutely necessary, although it too adds to the enjoyment of sexual relations.

If there is going to be a certain amount of what might be termed a growing sense of isolation among many people's lives in the 1990's and beyond, then we had better face this realistically. Friends, contemporaries, even spouses die as time passes. Now some people seem to have an urgent "need" for love and affection, that is, a need to receive it and a need to give it. But admitting one's <u>desire</u> for love and affection is <u>not</u> the same thing as saying that it is a <u>dire necessity</u> to be loved at all times. But it is a conclusion of mine, after listening to thousands of clients over many years, that *no one is ever loved <u>exactly</u> as they would <u>prefer</u> to be loved.* And we cannot <u>demand</u> that anyone love us completely and unwaveringly (and some even say, *spontaneously,* yet!) for the rest of our lives (at least not realistically expect our demands to rule the world!).

However, working to get as much of that wonderful stuff as one can is certainly realistic and healthy. But arbitrarily defining love as an absolute necessity in one's life is a self-defeating measure on anyone's part. And if there happen to be rather long periods during one's life when a loved one is not available ("dry spells"), that need not mean that one has to give up all sexual contacts. There are various legitimate and rational reasons why one might not wish to get married at various times in a lifetime. Still one might wish to have some sex during these same periods. And it is possible that one can find a partner with whom one might enjoy good sexual relations even though neither person loves the other. Affection would certainly help make the sex relations more enjoyable. But it seems to me that too many people are hung up on the concepts of love and sex and had better clarify their thinking on these important matters.

certainly help make the sex performance more enjoyable. But it is clear to me
that too many people are hung up on the concepts of love and sex and had
relationships their thinking of these important matters.

SUGGESTED FURTHER READING

Ard, Ben N., Jr. "Love and Aggression: The Perils of Loving," pp. 286 -295, *in* Ard, Ben N., Jr. & Ard, C. C. (Editors) *Handbook of Marriage Counseling.* Palo Alto: Science & Behavior Books, 2nd ed., 1976.

Ard, Ben Neal, Jr. *Rational Sex Ethics.* New York: Peter Lang, 2nd ed., 1989.

Bauer, Bernhard. *Woman and Love.* New York: Liveright, 2 volumes, 1927.

Callahan, Roger & Levine, Karen. *It Can happen To You: The Practical Guide to Romantic Love.* New York: A & W Publishers, 1982.

Curtin, Mary Ellen. (Editor) *Symposium on Love.* New York: Behavioral Publications, 1973.

Ellis, Albert. "Romantic Love," pp. 97-121, *in* Ellis, Albert. *The American Sexual Tragedy.* New York: Twayne, 1954.

Ellis, Albert. "The Justification of Sex Without Love," pp. 66-86, *in* Ellis, Albert. *Sex Without Guilt.* New York: Lyle Stuart, 1958.

Ellis, Albert. "On Myths About Love," pp. 159-167, *in* Ellis, Albert. *Sex Without Guilt.* New York: Lyle Stuart, 1958.

248

Ellis, Albert. *If This Be Sexual Heresy.* New York: Lyle Stuart, 1963.

Fromm, Erich. *The Art of Loving.* New York: Harper, 1956.

Grant, Vernon W. "Love, Sexual," pp. 646-656, *in* Ellis, Albert & Abarbanel, Albert. (Editors) *The Encyclopedia of Sexual Behavior.* New York: Hawthorn Books, Volume 2, 1961.

Kirch, A. M. (Editor) *The Anatomy of Love.* New York: Dell, 1960.

Loudin, Jo. *The Hoax of Romance.* Englewood Cliffs, N.J.: Prentice-Hall, 1981.

Maslow, A. H. *Motivation and Personality.* New York: Harper & Row, 2nd ed., 1970.

Montagu, Ashley. (Editor) *The Meaning of Love.* New York: Julian Press, 1953.

Suttie, I.D. *The Origins of Love and Hate.* London: Kegan Paul, 1935.

Vannoy, Russell. *Sex Without Love: A Philosophical Exploration.* Buffalo: Prometheus Books, 1980.

Young, Wayland. *Eros Denied.* New York: Grove Press, 1964.

"Thus, even if the acuteness of passion receedes, there remains enough of its glow to enrich the relationship with mutual respect, tenderness, and gratitude."

Therese Benedek
(Quoted in Krich, 160, p. 137)

CHAPTER 16

SEX IN THE LATER YEARS: IS IT ACCEPTABLE?

Looking ahead into the 1990's and beyond, if present trends continue, more and more people these days are living longer than in past centuries. And yet we continue to base our ideas about sex among the mature on concepts from thousands of years ago, rather than facing up to the newer scientific facts and what overall scientific evidence we now have. We had better help establish the right of older persons to express their sexuality freely and without fear or guilt. (Rubin, 1968)

Many aging males and females really need to be encouraged to continue an active sex life way beyond what they have heretofore assumed was "right" and/or "proper." Sexual life after sixty is possible, as Rubin (1965) has documented.

What are the facts? In the research data available, the intensity and duration of physiological responses of a sexual nature seem to be reduced with advancing years. That is, there is a reduction in sexual responsiveness in males over fifty; specifically, erection takes much longer and ejaculation lacks the same force and duration. But some males who maintain regularity of sexual expression, particularly with a healthy mental orientation, may extend their satisfying sexual life beyond the eighty-year age level.

Despite some loose talk of "climacteric" among males in some of the popular literature, in fact there is no point at which old age suddenly enters the picture among males. (Rubin, 1968, p. 519) Males do not have

252

anything comparable to the menopause in women, that is, a definite point occurring regularly in all men, when they are no longer able to sire any progeny.

Sudden total extinction of potency is not a normal manifestation of again among men. A few men in their seventies are still capable of frequent, vigorous, and sustained erections and sexual performance, sometimes even daily, although that is exceptional. As Daniel Wiener has put it,

"The male is often in for a particularly hard time psychologically because he undergoes no clear physical changes, even though many physicians refer to a "change of life" in the male as though it were as objective as it is in women. His sexual capacity declines only slowly until old age, and his glandular changes are very gradual. Without physiological referents, his concerns are more clearly psychological." (Daniel Wiener, *in* Broderick & Bernard, 1969, p. 332)

Probably the biggest problem for many people in our culture regarding sex in the later years is just accepting the fact that sex is appropriate, proper, and a fine thing, long after the reproductive aspect is past being a possibility for the woman. Too many people in our culture who follow the so-called "conventional wisdom" have equated sex with reproduction (a false legacy from religious teachings) and, after a woman's menopause insures that there will be no more reproduction, there frequently is an assumption that sex is "unseemly," if not out of order.

One older couple thought they were long past any possibility of pregnancy. The woman assumed she had completely passed through her menopause, which obviously was not the case, since she became pregnant. The couple then had quite different responses to the pregnancy. Since they were in their later years, with four grown sons, the woman was slightly embarrassed at the pregnancy. Her physician, because of her age, recommended a therapeutic abortion.

The husband in this case was pleased as punch at the pregnancy and wanted to brag about his potency to his friends. Obviously, sex in the later years means quite different things to different people.

If couples in the later years can get rid of some of their self-defeating assumptions that sex is not proper in the later years, they can then continue to enjoy sex in the last decades of their lives. Although the capacity for sexual response does seem to slow down gradually, sex can be enjoyed for a much longer period than our puritanical and victorian heritage would have us believe. (Ard, 1989)

Older people are entitled to enjoy sex as much as young people; they have the right to express their sexuality freely and without guilt. (Rubin, 1968) Fear and irrational ideas are the main impediments, although there are, realistically, physiological considerations also.

Men in their later years sometimes develop prostate problems (which obviously need checking out with a physician), and they sometimes after prostate operations, have retrograde ejaculations (i.e., they ejaculate back into the bladder rather than externally). I have had a hypothesis that if men continued an active sex life into their later years they would be less likely to have prostate problems. I would like to see this hypothesis explored with a good scientific research study.

Women in the later years may lose some of the moistness or

lubrication in the vagina during sexual excitement, but fortunately this can readily be replaced (e.g., with various lubricants which her physician can recommend). Other factors which increasing age brings in women are that reaction of the clitoris to direct stimulation may be somewhat delayed and the duration of orgasm may be reduced.

Older men sometimes notice that the ejaculatory jets gradually decrease in vigor and the ejaculate becomes scantier. Many men seem to require a somewhat longer period of intercourse to reach orgasm.

Just how to account for all the noted decrease in sexual activity in the later years is not a simple matter. There are probably many factors involved, both physiological and psychological. There is obviously a general decline in physiological capacity to some degree (which varies with different persons); there may also be something which might be called psychological fatigue, or loss of interest in repetition of the same sort of experience (when, perhaps, the possibilities of exploring new techniques have been exhausted with a particular partner), and then new types of contacts, new situations have frequently rearoused flagging sexual interests. Frankly speaking, monotony of a repetitious sexual relationship (usually translated into boredom with the particular partner) can also be a factor. If there is preoccupation with career or economic concerns, these can enter in and adversely affect sexual relations. If there have been increasing difficulties in sexual relations (or otherwise problems between the partners), there can arise a fear of failure (or just anticipation of an unsatisfying sexual experience) associated with previous contacts which can inhibit sexual performance or even sexual desire.

For both men and women, in my clinical experience, the problem of monotony (or psychological fatigue) may be an important factor in the aging person's loss of interest in sexual activity. In other words, over-familiarity may be a factor. Lack of sexual interest or enthusiasm on the part of either partner can have an adverse affect. The loss of personal attractiveness must also be mentioned. The harried partner who comes to breakfast (or bed) in an unattractive condition is practically a cliche around which many jokes have been framed but still occurs. The partner who skips showers, deodorants and mouthwash is another common occurrence. Both partners may lose interest in taking good care of their bodies, both as to muscle tone and cleanliness, for example.

Middle-aged men frequently are at the height of their careers and their intense involvement can act as a deterrent to sexual interest. I have had male clients turn to other women to talk about their career interests (and subsequently get involved in an extramarital sexual affair, which was not the primary motivation) because they reported their wives were not sufficiently interested in their (husband's) work. Visit any restaurant and watch the dinner conversation between the couples present. Too often one sees older couples merely sitting it out, or eating their meal in silence. Couples who have lived together so long that they have lost interest in each other as persons are hardly going to have great sex together when they get home from such a silent dinner.

Excessive alcoholic intake as well as taking many drugs can also adversely affect sexual performance at any age and is apparently increasing among both men and women in the later years. Men have had a long history of the use of alcohol; recently women have shown a striking increase in consuming it.

The "fear of failure" can enter into later sexual performance, particularly where the man has not been as successful either in his own eyes or in those of his partner. Many a man has, in effect, withdrawn from sexual activity because his partner has taunted him about declining sexual interest, or made caustic, sarcastic remarks at a cocktail party about his performance in bed (believe it or not, this is not a rare phenomenon). Once a man has an impotent experience, he may back off from later opportunities because he fears he is permanently impotent (i.e., that he will "fail" again and never be able to perform again). Obviously, better knowledge (see the earlier chapter on impotency) and professional consultation may be helpful in such instances.

Women in our culture face a particularly hard time in the later years because, for one thing, all the traits that our youth-oriented culture values so highly in the female seem to be vanishing in the older woman's view. That is, a woman's figure tends to lessen in attractiveness in the later years, what with the breasts sagging, lines appearing, stretch marks from bearing children, or just the natural results of aging may affect the woman's view of herself. Gray hair may not be much of a problem with the use of modern cosmetics, but many women in our culture give up sex because they feel they are no longer sexually attractive.

While sexual attractiveness is still important to many women in the later years, overemphasis on physical beauty and its natural decline can seriously interfere with an adequate sex life. Accepting what one cannot change is still major part of wisdom in mental health and one's sex life. Rather than giving up on one's sex life, one can recognize the importance of regular sexual activity.

As Rubin pointed out, "All authorities seem to agree that regularity of sexual activity is the essential factor in maintaining sexual capacity and performance for both males and females." (Rubin, 1968, p. 523) This would seem to be a good conclusion for all those in the later years (or even approaching them) to remember.

When older males have lost their sexual partners, in one way or another, many men report rapid loss of sexual tension and potency. Many older women have reported to me that when they have lost their sexual partners, in whatever fashion, they frequently seem to lose their interest in sex. So it might be bluntly concluded that it does not matter so much in what manner sexual expression has been employed as long as relatively high levels of activity are maintained. Continued sexual activity is good for one's health (both mental and physical) and it would be better to maintain one's sexual activity rather than merely allow it to die out because one has lost one's sexual partner. So rather than advising abstinence (as our religious teachings would have it), the wise counselor will instruct his clients about the importance of an active and continued sex life. (Rubin, 1968, p. 525) A good motto to remember might be: Use it or lose it!

And, for those older persons who cannot find a suitable person as a sexual partner, masturbation is an acceptable alternative (a valid form of sexual expression) until such a partner is available. This needs to be stressed, because many older people still have many irrational reservations against masturbation.

For some people in the later years, the sex drive may seem to lessen in intensity as a natural accompaniment of again, and therefore sexual expression may play more of a minor role in their later years than in their younger ones. But sometimes sex is given up in the later years unnecessarily, for irrational reasons. As Rubin has put it:

"However, when sexual desires and needs are repressed, distorted, or made unhealthy by negative attitudes arising from our general cultural prejudice against sexuality in later life, these desires may well consume a disproportionate amount of emotional energy and attention." (Rubin, 1968, p. 529)

Where this occurs, seeking professional help is clearly indicated. And where the person is willing to persistently do the hard work involved in questioning and challenging and getting rid of his or her irrational beliefs, then significant change can occur: it is never too late to learn.

In conclusion, I would like to report some of the positive findings of Abe Maslow regarding sex in the later years. Many researchers have reported that sex seems to deteriorate with increasing years, to some degree. I, too, have seen this in many clients. In seeking for explanations of this decline in sex in the later years some might hypothesize, as we have seen, that continued sexual experiences (of the same routine sort) with the same partner over the years naturally tend to deteriorate. A principle sometimes introduced is that "familiarity breeds contempt." There certainly is some evidence for this being true to some extent, as we have seen earlier. However, Maslow has found contradictory evidence among his self-actualizing (or psychologically healthy) people:

"Another finding that contradicts folk wisdom and also some of the more esoteric theorists on sexuality and love, is the definite indication that in self-actualizing people the quality of the love satisfactions and the sex satisfactions may both improve with the

length of the relationship. It seems quite clear that even the strictly sensual and physical satisfactions can be improved by familiarity with the partner rather than by novelty in healthy people." (Maslow, 1970, p. 184)

Maslow later added an afterthought which may help explain somewhat why his finding is not more universal. "I will say that the better people are, the more they will be loved with greater familiarity; the worse people are the *less* they will be liked as familiarity increases." (Maslow, 1970, p. 185)

Perhaps another way of saying the same thing, in a way, is to say that kindness, consideration, thoughtfulness, and affection can come to mean more than the curve of cheek or breast or ankle. If good sex involves the desire to please, to give as well as to get, then this more tender component may become more important as people grow older.

SUGGESTED FURTHER READING

Ard, Ben N., Jr. "Nothing's Uglier Than Sin," *Rational Living,* 2 (1971), 4-6.

DeMartino, Manfred F. "The Sexual Life of the Middle-Aged and the Aged," *in* DeMartino, Manfred F. (Editor) *Sexual Behavior and Personality Characteristics.* New York: Citadel Press, 1963, pp. 363-391.

Le Witter, Maximilian & Abarbanel, Albert. "Aging and Sex," *in* Ellis, Albert & Abarbanel, Albert (Editors) *The Encyclopedia of Sexual Behavior.* New York: Hawthorn Books, 1961, pp. 75-81.

Maslow, Abraham H. *Motivation and Personality.* New York: Harper & Row, 2nd edition, 1970.

Rubin, Isadore. *Sexual Life After Sixty.* New York: Basic Books, 1965.

Rubin, Isadore. "Sex and the Aging Man and Woman," *in* Vincent, Clark E. (Editor) *Human Sexuality in Medical Education and Practice.* Springfield, Illinois: Thomas, 1968, pp. 517-531.

Weiner, Daniel N. "Sexual Problems in Clinical Experience," *in* Broderick, Carlfred B. & Bernard, Jessie (Editors) *The Individual, Sex, and Society.* Baltimore: Johns Hopkins Press, 1969, pp. 317-341.

SUGGESTED FURTHER READING

"What disturbs men's minds is not events but their judgments on events . . .And so when we are hindered, or disturbed, or distressed, let us never lay the blame on others, but on ourselves, that is, on our own judgments. To accuse others for one's own misfortunes is a sign of want of education; to accuse oneself shows that one's education has begun; to accuse neither oneself nor others shows that one's education is complete."

Epictetus

CHAPTER 17

EPILOGUE:
ADOPTING A RATIONAL,
SCIENTIFIC APPROACH TO SEX

In the preceding chapters I have tried to show how one psychologist, sexologist, and marriage counselor has worked toward resolving certain sexual problems in a variety of clients. Obviously in a brief introduction such as contained in this book, one cannot realistically treat all the possible sexual problems extensively. If a person wanted to go into detail, the verbatim case reports could fill many chapters by themselves. I have, in another context, presented, for example, such a case report involving masochism. (Ard, 1971b) Here, I have presented what might be termed vignettes or brief case discussions to illustrate just what sort of things go on in the counseling and psychotherapy which deals with such sexual problems.

I have tried to give the interested reader some idea of how one therapist works. (Ard, 1971a) The reader who is interested in more detail may wish to consult some of my other writings. (Ard, 1968; Ard, 1969; Ard, 1973) Basically, at this point, by way of brief summary, one might say that the approach used with the various clients and their sexual problems in the preceding pages was a deeply philosophical kind of psychotherapy, one that was active, direct, rational, reasonable, scientific, persuasive, and humanistic. This rational-emotive therapy has been most extensively discussed and explained by Dr. Albert Ellis, who originated and developed

266

this approach with contributions from other colleagues. (Albert Ellis, 1973; Ellis & Grieger, 1977, 1986; Ellis, et al, 1971)

The "opposition," or the ultimate source of a lot of the indoctrination with the irrational ideas, beliefs and assumptions many clients have received, which basically caused them to have the sexual problems, may be traced to our conventional code of morality regarding sex, that is, in our culture, the Judeo-Christian religious tradition (with its overtones of puritanical and victorian views of sex). I have documented this hypothesis in other books. (Ard, *Living Without Guilt and/or Blame: Conscience, Superego and Psychotherapy,* 1983; Ard, *Rational Sex Ethics,* 1989) Now some readers may question this conclusion, and they are encouraged to check it out by reading more of the various authors cited, and not just take my word for it. But if clients are to achieve better mental health (within which I would assume a healthier attitude toward sex would be well integrated), they frequently had better learn how to re-think in a more scientific, logical fashion, the various irrational ideas and assumptions which ultimately have come from their religious indoctrination. (Ard, 1972b) Even people who are not religious (i.e., do not go to church or perhaps do not recall ever being taught formally anything about religion or even sex), frequently derive their philosophy of life (particularly with regard to sex) from the code to which our culture gives its lip service, although not its behavior. So even the nonreligious person (so-called) is greatly influenced into believing a lot of irrational nonsense merely by being reared in our culture.

Such religious teachings as exemplified by Billy Graham, Oral Roberts, the late Rev. Jim Jones, Dan Smoot, the right-wing Birchers, and other fundamentalist sects are still very influential in our culture even as we near the 21st century, particularly influencing legislatures, schools, and colleges and universities. Even some psychologists, such as Mowrer, for example, have sought to increase feelings of sin and guilt in clients, despite the fact that such feelings rarely, if ever, helped anyone solve sexual problems in a rational way. (Ard, 1967a)

The therapeutic approach I have suggested (rational-emotive therapy or RET for short) is better than some of the more traditional approaches and one that gets the client to see that he is having sexual problems because of his belief system; that is, he keeps reindoctrinating himself with irrational beliefs which are very self-defeating. (Ellis, 1973) In simple A-B-C terms (a useful scheme for separating the concepts involved), it is rarely what the client may assume is the activating event ("A") that directly causes the client the emotional consequences ("C") that are so self-defeating. These activating events are usually external to the client and frequently deep in his past (and therefore he seems to have no control over them or any responsibility for them). But what the client can learn to understand is that nearly always (in the kinds of sexual and psychological problems we have been considering in this book) and intermediary step ("B"), which is the client's belief system. In the B step the client, in effect (either consciously or unconsciously), tells himself something detrimental and irrational, or assumes something is awful or catastrophic, and it is this B step or belief system that really causes the problem.

When a client can be encouraged or persuaded to challenge and question some of these irrational beliefs, values, premises, or assumptions, and get rid of them (frequently by acting in ways that, outside the therapy hour, challenge his assumptions, doing what have been called in RET

268

"homework assignments"), he can usually discover that what he has irrationally feared is not quite as bad as he assumed (he stops assuming and learns to check things out scientifically and empirically). There are usually alternatives that he has not thought of that can be tried, once he has questioned his irrational assumptions or philosophy of life (specifically dealing with, in many cases, ideas about sex, love, marriage, the other sex, masculinity, femininity, and the like). Frequently the therapist had better get the client to alter his habitual ways of making moral judgments - in laymen's terms frequently thought of as the voice of conscience (or in psychoanalytic terms, his superego) - which may be the basic cause of his sexual problems. (Ard, 1972a)

The client, if he wants to integrate sex in his life in a manner which will be satisfying and not self-defeating, had better develop a more rational, humanistic, scientific philosophy of life. I have discussed such a philosophy at length in several publications. (Ard, 1965; Ard, 1967b; Ard, 1972b) Suffice it to say here that the therapist does not arbitrarily impose any particular philosophy of life, but through a kind of Socratic dialogue, with occasional confrontations, and with many probing questions, gets the client to reexamine his previous philosophy of life and sex and see where it is self-defeating and therefore needs changing. The unexamined life is indeed hardly worth living. The client had better learn to de-indoctrinate himself (sometimes with the professional help of the therapist) and then he can be re-educated, that is, learn to think and read critically and scientifically and develop a more enlightened self-interest. This is long-term hedonism of a humanistic variety with a scientific base. The details each person can work out for himself, taking into consideration his particular circumstances, age, health, goals, and so on. (Wiener, 1968) The open mind works out better than the closed mind. That is a hypothesis I have developed over the years which I urge the readers to check out for themselves.

For those readers who, after reading this book, might like to consider getting some further professional help with some of their sexual problems, I will mention several referral resources. For some names of qualified rational-emotive therapists in your area, you may contact

Institute for Rational-Emotive Therapy
45 East 65th Street
New York, N.Y. 10021
(212) 535-0822

For some names of some qualified sex therapists near your area, contact

American Association of Sex Educators,
Counselors and Therapists
Eleven Dupont Circle, N. W., Suite 220
Washington, D.C. 20036-1207
(202) 461-1171

For some names of some qualified marriage counselors in your area, contact

American Association for Marriage and Family Therapy
1717 K Street (Suite 407)
Washington, D.C. 20006
(202) 429-1825

It is never too late to learn some more about how one thinks feels and acts about sex, love and marriage problems.

SUGGESTED FURTHER READING

Ard, Ben N., Jr. "A Psychologist's View of Humanism," *Progressive World,*
20 (1965), 34-43.

Ard, Ben N., Jr. "Nothing's Uglier Than Sin," *Rational Living,* 2, 1 (1967a),
4-6

Ard, Ben N., Jr. "Are You A Humanist?" *Progressive World,* 21 (1967b),
23-33.

Ard, Ben N., Jr. "The A-B-C of Marriage Counseling," *Rational Living,* 2,
2 (1968), 10-12

Ard, Ben N., Jr. "A Rational Approach to Marriage Counseling," *in* Ard,
Ben N., Jr. & Ard, C. C. (Editors) *Handbook of Marriage
Counseling.* Palo Alto: Science & Behavior Books, 1969, 115-127.

Ard, Ben N., Jr. "The Therapist as a Person (Or: The Complete Counselor),
Marriage Counseling Quarterly, 6, 4 (1971a), 1-5.

Ard, Ben N., Jr. "The Case of the Black and Silver Masochist," *in* Ellis,
Albert et al (Editor) *Growth Through Reason: Verbatim Cases in
Rational-Emotive Therapy.* Palo Alto: Science & Behavior Books,
1971b, pp. 15-45.

Ard, Ben N., Jr. "The Conscience or Superego in Marriage Counseling," *in* Silverman, H. L. (Editor) *Marital Therapy.* Springfield, Illinois: Thomas, 1972a, pp. 237-244.

Ard, Ben N., Jr. "Mental Health and Religion," *Rational Living,* 78 (1972b), 7-12.

Ard, Ben N., Jr. *Living Without Guilt and/or Blame: Conscience, Superego and Psychotherapy.* Smithtown, N.Y.: Exposition Press, 1983.

Ard, Ben Neal, Jr. *Rational Sex Ethics.* New York: Peter Lang, 2nd ed., 1989.

Ellis, Albert, et al (Editor) *Growth Through Reason: Verbatim Cases in Rational-Emotive Therapy.* Palo Alto: Science & Behavior Books, 1971.

Ellis, Albert & Grieger, Russell, et al. *Handbook of Rational-Emotive Therapy.* New York: Springer, Volume 1, 1977, Volume 2, 1986.

Wiener, Daniel N. *A Practical Guide to Psychotherapy.* New York: Harper & Row, 1968.

"But words are things, and a small drop of ink,

Falling, like dew, upon a thought, produces

That which makes thousands, perhaps millions, think."

Don Juan, canto iii. st. 88

GLOSSARY

ABORTION:

The removal of a fetus from the uterus before it is viable. "Spontaneous abortion" is sometimes called "miscarriage" and means abortion not deliberately induced but occurring itself. "Therapeutic abortion" is a legal operation performed by a qualified physician.

ABSTINENCE:

Refraining from sexual intercourse. Whether this is detrimental or not has been a controversial issue. Complete abstinence for prolonged periods *does* indicate a deviation from normal development.

ADULTERY:

Sexual intercourse between a married person and an individual other than his or her legal spouse.

ANHEDONIA:

Lack of sexual desire.

APHRODISIAC:

Anything that is reputed to stimulate sexual desire (e.g., a drug or food).

BESTIALITY:

Sexual relations with animals. Sometimes called zoophilia.

BIGAMY:

Being married to more than one spouse at the same time (i.e., illegally).

BIRTH CONTROL:

Deliberate limitation of the number of children born-through contraceptives, the pill, IUDs, diaphragms, etc.

BISEXUALITY:

Having sexual relations with both sexes; a concept of psychoanalytic theory not accepted by all authorities.

BUGGERY:

Any type of sexual relations considered "abnormal" according to legal definitions; both buggery and sodomy have been used to describe sexual relations between a human and an animal; sodomy refers to the insertion of the penis into the rectum.

"CHANGE OF LIFE":

See CLIMACTERIC; MENOPAUSE.

CIRCUMCISION:

Surgical removal of the foreskin or prepuce of the male penis, usually done soon after birth.

CLIMACTERIC:

Menopause ("change of life"); the syndrome of physical and psychological changes that occur at the termination of menstrual function (i.e., the loss of reproduction capability).

CLIMAX:

See ORGASM.

CLITORAL ORGASM:

Orgasm achieved primarily by stimulation of the clitoris;

some authorities say "orgasm is orgasm, however achieved." Contrasted by some with "vaginal orgasm."

CLITORIS:

A small, very sensitive, erectile body situated just above the urethral opening and in the upper angle of the vagina; the main seat of sensuous feeling in the female; the clitoris becomes erect during sexual excitement.

COITUS:

Sexual intercourse between male and female, in which the male penis is inserted into the female vagina.

"COMING OUT":

Gay vernacular term to refer acknowledging to oneself and to others that one's sexual orientation (or preference) is homosexual.

CONDOM:

A contraceptive used by males consisting usually of a rubber sheath that is drawn over the erect penis before coitus. It acts to protect from venereal disease and also acts as a form of birth control.

COPROPHILIA:

A morbid interest in feces.

COPULATION:

Sexual intercourse; coitus.

CRABS:

An itchy skin irritation in the genital area caused by the bites of the crab louse.

CUNNILINGUS:
> The act of using the tongue or mouth in erotic play with the external female genitalia (vulva).

DEFLORATION:
> The rupture of the hymen in a virgin's first experience of coitus.

DEMI-VIRGIN:
> A "technical" virgin who frequently has done every sexual act imaginable except allowing the penis in the vagina.

DEPO-PROVERA:
> The trade name of a hormone manufactured by Upjohn in the United States. It has several clinical applications, one of which is to help sex offenders gain personal governance of their sexual conduct.

DETUMESCENCE:
> The decreasing of the body's erectile tissue in the genitals (e.g., the penis) following orgasm.

DIABETES:
> A disease characterized by an excessive formation of sugar in the blood; sometimes can affect sexual performance.

DIAPHRAGM:
> A birth control device, a rubber contraceptive, used by women.

DOUCHE:
> A stream of water or other liquid solution directed into

the female vagina for sanitary, medical, or contraceptive reasons. Authorities differ on its value.

"DOWNER":

A street term applied to barbiturates and other depressants.

DYSMENORRHEA:

Painful menstruation.

EJACULATION:

The expulsion of the male semen (or ejaculate) usually at the climax (orgasm) of the male's performance of the sexual act.

ENDOCRINOLOGIST:

A physician who specializes in disease and disorders of the endocrine glands.

EROGENOUS ZONES:

A sexually sensitive area of the body: e.g., the mouth, lips, breasts, nipples, genitals; varies in different people.

EXHIBITIONISM:

Problematic sexual behavior in which the individual, usually male, suffers from a compulsion to expose his genitals publicly.

FELLATIO:

The act of taking the penis into the mouth and sucking it.

FETISHISM:

Problematic sexual behavior in which sexual gratification

280

is achieved by means of an object (e.g., an article of clothing, such as women's lingerie, or shoes, or the like) that bears sexual symbolism for the individual.

"FISTING":

A vernacular term for the sexual practice of inserting the hand and/or forearm into the rectum or vagina.

FOREPLAY:

The preliminary stages of sexual intercourse in which the partners stimulate each other by kissing, touching, caressing,a and so on.

FORNICATION:

Sexual intercourse between an unmarried male and female.

"FRIGIDITY":

Coldness, indifference, or disinterestedness on the part of a woman to sexual intercourse or sexual stimulation; inability to experience sexual pleasure or gratification.

FROTTAGE:

Rubbing against an individual of the other sex, usually a stranger, e.g., in a subway or elevator.

"GAY":

Homosexual; the homosexual subculture is sometimes referred to as the "gay life," as contrasted to the "straight" world of heterosexuals.

GENDER-IDENTITY/ROLE:

Gender identity is the private experience of gender role, and gender role is the public manifestation of gender identity.

GONORRHEA:

One of the most common of the venereal diseases; it is caused by the gonococcus.

GYNECOLOGIST:

A physician who specializes in the treatment of diseases of the female reproductive and sexual organs.

HALLUCINOGENIC DRUG:

A drug (e.g., LSD, marijuana, STP, and the like) that produces hallucinations or the perception of things (sights and sounds) that are not actually present.

HOMOPHOBIA:

(adj. HOMOPHOBIC) The condition in which those whose lifestyle is homosexual are dreaded and feared.

HOMOPHILIA:

(adj. HOMOPHILIC) Love of the same sex (homosexuality); approval of the homosexual lifestyle.

HOMOSEXUALITY:

Sexual activity with members of one's own sex.

HOT FLASHES:

The flushing and perspiring which frequently accompanies the change of life (menopause) in women.

HYMEN:

The "maidenhead"; the membranous fold that partly covers the external opening of the vagina in most (but not all) virgin females.

HYSTERECTOMY:

Surgical removal of the uterus in females.

IMPOTENCY:

Inability to achieve or maintain an erection sufficient for purposes of actual intercourse.

INTROMISSION:

The insertion of the male penis into the female vagina.

INVERSION:

Homosexuality.

LESBIAN:

A female homosexual.

LIBIDO:

Sexual impulse (instinct), drive, or urge in psychoanalytic theory; a broader concept than mere sex.

"LOVEMAP":

A developmental representation or template in the mind and in the brain depicting the idealized lover, the idealized love affair, and the idealized program of sexuoerotic activity projected in imagery or actual engaged in with that lover. (John Money's concept.)

LSD:

Lysergic acid diethylamide, or "acid"; causes distortion of the senses and also distorts the sexual experience.

MARRIAGE COUNSELOR:

A professionally trained person with an advanced graduate degree (master's or Ph.D.) who has studied how to treat

love, sex and marital problems. Licensed in some but not
all states.

MAIDENHEAD:

The hymen.

MARIJUANA:

A drug which causes varying degrees of distortion of
hearing, taste, touch, and sight; despite its reputed
aphrodisiac effects, there is no evidence of an increased
physical effect on sexuality.

MASOCHISM:

Problematic sexual behavior wherein a person seems to
derive sexual gratification from having pain inflicted.

MASTURBATION:

Self-stimulation of the genitals, usually to climax;
autoeroticism.

MENOPAUSE:

The period of cessation of menstruation in the human
female, occurring usually between the ages of forty-five
and fifty-five; climacteric; "change of life."

MENSTRUATION:

The discharge of blood from the uterus through the
vagina that normally recurs at approximately four-week
intervals in women between the ages of puberty and
menopause.

MONOGAMY:

Life-long marriage between one man and one woman, with

284

no extramarital sex.

NECKING:

Kissing the lips and face of one's sexual partner; see PETTING, which usually means caresses extended below the neck.

NECROPHILIA:

A morbid sexual attraction to corpses.

NOCTURNAL EMISSION:

An involuntary male ejaculation during sleep; a "wet dream."

NYMPHOMANIA:

Excessive sexual desire in a woman, resulting in compulsive (indiscriminate) sex which frequently brings little satisfaction to the woman.

OBSESSION:

The persistent recurrence of some irrational thought or idea, or an attachment to (or fixation on) a particular individual or object.

ONANISM:

Withdrawal of the male penis from the female vagina before ejaculation; also know as coitus interruptus; erroneously equated in some people's minds with masturbation.

ORGASM:

The peak or climax of sexual excitement in sexual activity. Some authorities distinguish between "clitoral" and "vaginal" orgasm in women; others say "orgasm is orgasm, however attained."

PARAPHILIA:
Problematic sexual behavior; also sometimes known as sexual deviation or aberrant sexual activity.

PATHOLOGICAL:
Pertaining to a diseased, disturbed or abnormal physical or mental condition.

PEDERASTY:
Male sexual relations with a boy; also sexual relations via the anus.

PENIS ENVY:
Freud's psychoanalytic concept (or assumption) that females envy the male's possession of a penis. Some say it is more properly conceived as envy of the male role.

PERVERSION:
Old term for sexual deviation from the normal; paraphilia.

PETTING:
Sexual contact usually involving touching, caressing (below the neck), usually thought of as sexual foreplay but frequently excluding coitus, although it can be done to orgasm.

PHIMOSIS:
Tightness of the foreskin of the male penis, so that it cannot be drawn back over the glans; an analogous condition is said by some to exist with the clitoris.

POLYANDRY:

The form of marriage in which one woman has more than one husband at a time.

POLYGAMY:

The form of marriage in which a spouse of either sex may possess a plurality of mates at the same time.

POLYGYNY:

The form of marriage in which one man has more than one wife at the same time.

PREMATURE EJACULATION:

Ejaculation or "coming" prior to intromission or immediately after intromission.

PREPUCE:

Foreskin.

PRIAPISM:

Persistent abnormal erection of the penis in males, usually without sexual desire.

PROGESTERONE:

The female hormone (sometimes known as the pregnancy hormone).

PROMISCUITY:

Engaging in sexual intercourse indiscriminately with many persons; conservatives equate it with *any* premarital or extramarital sex whatsoever (obviously a rather arbitrary definition).

PROSTATE:

The gland in the male that surrounds the urethra and neck of the bladder.

PROSTATITIS:

Inflammation of the prostate gland, typically a disease of older men.

PRUDISH:

Extremely or falsely modes, especially about sexual matters; characterized by a repudiation of sex and anything connected with sexuality.

PSYCHEDELIC DRUGS:

Hallucinogenic drugs, mind-altering drugs (e.g., LSD, acid, speed, STP, PCP, barbiturates, amphetamines, marijuana, and so on).

PSYCHIATRIST:

A physician (M.D.) specializing in treatment of mental illness.

PSYCHOANALYSIS:

A system of treatment, originated by Sigmund Freud and others, that tries to alleviate emotional disorders by means of unconscious factors that are revealed, supposedly, by dreams and "free associations." Ordinarily takes several or many years.

PSYCHOGENIC:

A symptom that has a psychological origin; functional as contrasted with organic.

PSYCHOLOGIST:

A licensed specialist, usually with a Ph.D. degree, whose basic training is in human behavior (normal and abnormal), who may do counseling and psychotherapy with people who have problems involving sex, love, or marriage.

PURITANICAL:

Manifesting the influence of Puritan beliefs or practices; morally strict, prone to inveigh against current practices, wherein pleasure is bad; the "haunting fear that someone, somewhere, may be happy." (H. L. Mencken)

REFRACTORY PERIOD:

A temporary state of physiological resistance to sexual stimulation immediately following an orgasmic experience; usually longer in males than in females (term used by Masters and Johnson).

RELIGION:

As used in this book, faith unfounded on fact; usually involves belief in, and dependence upon, a supernatural being (God).

RET:

Rational-emotive therapy, originated by Dr. Albert Ellis in the 1950's. An effective and elegant form of brief therapy that gets at the client's philosophic beliefs, frequently irrational, that cause problems in living, common in sexual problems.

RETROGRADE EJACULATION:
> Backward ejaculation in males into the posterior urethra and bladder, instead of into the anterior urethra and out through the meatus of the penis. Occurs after prostate surgery.

"RHYTHM METHOD":
> A so-called method of birth control that relies on the presumed "safe period" or infertile days in the woman's menstrual cycle; not very reliable; sometimes referred to as the "Russian roulette" method of birth control.

SADISM:
> The achieving of "pleasure" (or sexual gratification) by inflicting pain upon the sexual partner; problematic sexual behavior.

"SAFE PERIOD":
> The interval of the menstrual cycle when the female is *presumably* not ovulating; affected by a lot of factors such as climate, travel, psychological problems, stress, and so forth, and therefore not as "safe" as some people have supposed and have the children to prove it.

SAPPHISM:
> Another term for lesbianism or female homosexuality; Sappho was a Greek poetess who lived on the island of Lesbos.

SATYRIASIS:
> Insatiable sexual desire in men; the word derives from the

satyr of ancient Greek mythology, a figure half-man and half-goat, who symbolized fertility and lust.

SCOPOPHILIA: (or SCOPTOPHILIA):

Achieving sexual gratification by observing others in the nude; also known as VOYEURISM; the male who does this is sometimes called a "peeping Tom."

SEXUAL PSYCHOPATH:

A sex criminal; a legal term usually applied to confirmed and aggressive rapists, child molesters, sadists, "sex murderers," and so on.

SEXOLOGY:

The scientific study of sex; the treatment of sexual problems and disorders (a SEXOLOGIST is one who treats such problems).

SIMULTANEOUS ORGASM:

Climax of both partners at the same time; sometimes arbitrarily defined as the *only* satisfactory completion of the sex act (a very self-defeating notion).

SODOMY:

An act in which the penis is inserted into the partner's anus.

"SPANISH FLY":

A supposed aphrodisiac which actually does not cause sexual stimulation but rather irritates the sex organs.

"SPEED":

A slang term for amphetamines, drugs that stimulate the

central nervous system. Harmful and lead to unfortunate consequences.

"SUBLIMATION":

A psychoanalytic notion, subscribed to by many religious people, too, that one can satisfy sexual needs by nonsexual means (e.g., through painting, sculpture, exercise, and the like); an assumption which has little scientific validity.

SUPEREGO:

The psychoanalytic concept denoting the largely unconscious internalized prohibitions of parents and society learned early in life; somewhat analogous (but not exactly equivalent) to the conscience.

TESTOSTERONE:

The male testicular hormone that induces and maintains the male secondary sex characteristics.

TRANSEXUALISM
(sometimes TRANSSEXUALISM):

A compulsion or obsession to become a member of the other sex through surgical changes and hormonal treatment. The condition of crossing over to live full-time in the role of the other sex, with hormonal and surgical sex reassignment.

TRANSVESTISM:

Problematic sexual behavior characterized by a compulsive desire to wear the garments of the other sex; cross dressing in the clothes and style of the other sex.

TUMESCENCE:

The filling of the blood vessels of the genital organs causing swelling (in the male, an erection).

URETHRA:

The duct through which the urine passes from the bladder and is excreted outside the body.

URETHRITIS:

Inflammation of the urethra.

UROLOGIST:

A physician specializing in the medical treatment of the diseases and disorders of the urinary tract of both sexes, as well as the genital tract of the male.

UTERUS:

The womb; the hollow, pear-shaped organ in females within which the fetus develops.

VAGINAL ORGASM:

A debatable term. In some quarters, referring to an orgasm that a woman can achieve vaginally (with penis in the vagina, through normal sexual intercourse), as contrasted with "clitoral orgasm" (achieved through clitoral stimulation).

VAGINISMUS:

Recurrent premature contractions of the musculature of the vagina before intercourse, so that it is too tight and too dry to receive the penis.

VAS DEFERENS:

The sperm duct(s) in males, leading from the epididymis to the seminal vesicles and the urethra.

VASECTOMY:

A surgical procedure for sterilizing the male, involving the cutting or removal of a portion of the vas deferens, preventing sperm from being a part of the ejaculation.

VICTORIAN:

Typical or moral standards or conduct of the age of Queen Victoria, stuffy, hypocritical.

VOYEURISM:

Achieving sexual gratification by observing others in the nude or undressing; also known as scopophilia (the man who does this is frequently called a "peeping Tom.")

VULVA:

The external sex organs of the female.

"WET DREAM":

An involuntary ejaculation during sleep.

ZOOPHILIA:

See BESTIALITY.

INDEX

300

302